7 Keys to Spiritual Wellness

Other Loyola Press books by Joe Paprocki

The Bible Blueprint: A Catholic's Guide to Understanding and Embracing God's Word

Los planos de Biblia: Una guía católica para entender y acoger la Palabra de Dios

The Catechist's Toolbox: How to Thrive as a Religious Education Teacher

La caja de herramientas del catequista: Cómo triunfar en el ministerio de la educatión religiosa

Living the Mass: How One Hour a Week Can Change Your Life with Fr. Dominic Grassi

Practice Makes Catholic: Moving from a Learned Faith to a Lived Faith

A Well-Built Faith: A Catholic's Guide to Knowing and Sharing What We Believe

Una Fe Bien Construida: Guía católica para conocer y compartir lo que creemos

7 KEYS *to*
Spiritual WELLNESS

*Enriching Your Faith
by Strengthening the
Health of Your Soul*

JOE PAPROCKI, DMin

LOYOLA PRESS.
A JESUIT MINISTRY
Chicago

LOYOLA PRESS.
A JESUIT MINISTRY

3441 N. Ashland Avenue
Chicago, Illinois 60657
(800) 621-1008
www.loyolapress.com

Cover art: © iStockphoto/ThinkStock.

Library of Congress Cataloging-in-Publication Data

Paprocki, Joe.
  7 keys to spiritual wellness : enriching your faith by strengthening the health of your soul /
by Joe Paprocki.
      pages cm.
  Includes bibliographical references.
  ISBN-13: 978-0-8294-3689-1
  ISBN-10: 0-8294-3689-8
1. Spiritual life--Christianity. I. Title.
  BV4501.3.P36 2012
  248.4--dc23

                                                                        2011046895

Printed in the United States of America.

12 13 14 15 16 17 Bang 10 9 8 7 6 5 4 3 2 1

To my mom, the most
spiritually healthy person I
have ever known.

Contents

Introduction

Are you looking for more?

The spiritual life begins with this question. To be a spiritual person means to thirst for that "something more." Spiritual health is found through quenching that thirst for something deeper by drinking from the right cup.

Just as the body's immune system is strengthened by proper care (diet, exercise, handling stress, taking supplements), our spiritual wellness relies on balance and harmony. Without that balance we can find ourselves settling for less instead of striving for something more. Thankfully, we have a Divine Physician, Jesus Christ, who offers us a spiritual path to follow that promises to heal and restore us to spiritual wellness.

Spiritual wellness enables us to find "the more" that we seek. Unfortunately, for many people Christianity has come to be seen less as a spiritual path and more as a code of ethics. Christianity does indeed involve a moral code, but at the core of Jesus' Good News is an invitation to walk a spiritual path that leads to intimacy with our Creator. Simply put, Christian spirituality rests on the fact that God—who is the "more" that our hearts desire—is accessible through Jesus Christ and his living word. It's time for us to recover the spirituality of the Christian message, enabling followers of Jesus to experience the spiritual wellness Jesus promised when he said, "Peace I leave with you. My peace I give to you" (John 14:27).

In order to maintain spiritual wellness our soul needs to be fed, exercised, and cared for properly. God has provided us with what we need to ensure our spiritual health through seven enduring and reliable strategies that flow from Christian tradition. Here are the keys to spiritual wellness:

- Key One: Seeing Yourself As You Really Are
- Key Two: Actively Seeking the Good of Others
- Key Three: Thinking Before Acting
- Key Four: Holding on Loosely
- Key Five: Recognizing and Setting Limits
- Key Six: Seeking Beauty
- Key Seven: Unleashing Your Imagination

Entering into the spiritual life is best done by asking questions. To that end, I offer seven questions which correspond to the keys above. These questions open the door to the world of a deeper spirituality.

- Who's your court jester?
- What do you have that cannot be taken away?
- Is that your final answer?
- What's your security blanket?
- What scratches your itch?

- Where is your dream vacation spot?
- What gives you heartburn?

I believe these are perhaps the seven most provocative and important questions you will ever ask yourself. They hold the key to drinking from the right cup that will give you the nourishment needed to maintain spiritual health. In the pages ahead we will explore these seven questions and look at their enduring and reliable answers. My prayer is that upon completing this book, you will embrace Jesus' path to spiritual wellness, for only he can strengthen your soul's immune system and enable you to enjoy "the more" you so earnestly seek.

"If any one thirst, let him come to me and drink."

—John 10:37

Seeing Yourself As
You Really Are

Who's your court jester?

Everyone needs a court jester. And I'm not just talking about someone who can make you laugh. I mean someone who can make you laugh *at yourself.* In medieval monarchies, the court jester was more than a mere buffoon; he was a voice of common sense, insight, and honesty—often brutal honesty, as in "the truth hurts." He was the only person in the monarch's court who had license to mock the monarch, usually to reveal the folly of his or her majesty's ways. Richard Rohr minces no words when he describes the court jester as the only person who could tell the king that he was full of @#%&, and do so with impunity.

So I ask again, who's your court jester? Who gets to tell you that you're full of @#%&, and can get away with it because you know they love you? Who gets to reveal the folly of your ways and still receive an invitation to dinner? Perhaps it's a spouse, a sibling, one of your own children, a friend, or coworker. Without a court jester, we run the risk of believing the hype about ourselves. Without a court jester, we run the risk of not being able to attain a true and healthy self-image. And without a healthy self-image, our spiritual wellness is in jeopardy.

Achieving a healthy self-perception can seem as precarious as walking on a tightrope—it is a matter of balance. On the one hand, we are made in the image and likeness of God, and the affirmations we receive in life can help us to recognize our family resemblance to God. On the other hand, we are not God. We simply resemble God. And so our challenge is to find a balance that gives us a healthy self-esteem. Without balance, we run the risk of developing a distorted sense of self that can ultimately skew our perception of reality, including how we perceive others and God. Our quest is to be authentic—to see ourselves as we really are.

Look at me!

Unfortunately, the kind of self-criticism that leads to clear thinking about who we are is not in vogue in contemporary society. In fact, quite the opposite is true. Tootin' your own horn has become the norm in our society. Nowhere is this self-promotion more evident than in professional sports, especially football. Nowadays touchdowns, quarterback sacks, and other big plays are followed by animated displays of strutting, chest-thumping, and jawing. The message is clear: "I am better than you are!"

Politicians, actors, musicians, and celebrities of all kinds use every opportunity to promote themselves. (You may recall actor Charlie Sheen's response to the question of whether he was on drugs: "I'm on a drug. It's called Charlie Sheen.") Popular reality television shows document the mundane comings and goings of people's everyday lives. It is estimated that over 100 million people (including Yours Truly) have blogs, where they can position themselves as an expert and espouse their opinions on any topic—for once, getting the last word in. Popular Catholic blogger Mark Shea explains, tongue-in-cheek, that the reason for writing his blog, *Catholic and Enjoying It!* is "so that no thought of mine, no matter how stupid, should ever go unpublished again!" Not surprisingly, William Bennett's *The Book of Virtues* (a *New York Times* best seller and a popular book among evangelical Christians in the 1990s), fails to include the topic of humility in its discussion of traditional Christian values in Western Civilization. I guess he wouldn't have felt comfortable self-promoting his book if it dealt with humility.

Spiritual wellness and tooting your own horn are incompatible. So, the first key to spiritual wellness is to avoid the temptation to toot our own horns, lest we begin thinking we are more important than we really are. While it's true that we all need a healthy self-esteem, one of the greatest obstacles to spiritual wellness is self-esteem that has been overfed. We have an obesity problem in our society, and it's not limited to physical weight. Our egos are becoming alarmingly obese. So what's the big danger of having a swelled head? Simply put, it distorts our self-image, and the plain truth is that *you simply cannot be happy unless you see yourself as you truly are.*

Being put in your place

Tootin' your own horn used to be frowned upon. In ancient Greece the gods took care of humans who became a bit too arrogant. To the Greeks, good fortune was distributed proportionately to each individual according to what he or she deserved. When this proportion was disturbed, most often by an individual who believed that he or she possessed more good fortune than others (an attitude known to the Greeks as *hubris,* or in Christian tradition, *pride*), it caused a backlash of resentment among the gods. It was the job of the mythological goddess Nemesis to dole out retribution. She put things back into balance by punishing such individuals, thus putting them in their place.

In many cultures initiation rites are used to socialize the individual to take on a collective identity rather than an individual one. Often, these initiation rites include some form of pain and humiliation (a practice continued today to some degree in fraternity/sorority initiations on college campuses). This ritual strengthens the resolve of the individual and symbolizes the initiate's "death" as an individual and "rebirth" as a member of the collective. In other words, they are being told that their self-esteem comes from their membership in the community, not from individual accomplishments. In his book *Rites and Symbols of Initiation,* author Mircea Eliade explains that these initiation rites represent a culture's belief that "a man is made—he does not make himself all by himself." The bottom line is this: no self-promotion is allowed!

Sadly, we don't have many of these safeguards against self-promotion today in our country. One of the last is found in America's pastime, good old-fashioned baseball. In baseball, if a player hits a home run, pauses to admire its flight, and then struts around the bases thumping his chest and jawing at the pitcher, you can be sure that the next time up to bat, the first pitch he'll see will be a 95-mile-an-hour fastball in his ear or right under his chin (referred to as "chin music"). The message? Don't toot your own horn.

"God's doing real good"

Theologian and storyteller Jack Shea shares a good story about being put in your place.

It is known by everyone who cares to know that the Lord Jesus and St. Peter used to repair to the local tavern after a hard day of ministry to break bread and drink wine together.

On a certain rainy night, St. Peter turned to the Lord Jesus and grinned, "We're doing real good."

"We?" said the Lord Jesus.

Peter was silent. "All right, you're doing real good," he finally said.

"Me?" said the Lord Jesus.

Peter pondered a second time. "All right, God's doing real good," he finally admitted.

But the Lord Jesus saw how reluctant St. Peter was to admit the source of all goodness. He laughed and hit the table with glee.

The story continues as Peter complains that he is not getting his due. He tells Jesus he is going to prove how good he is by taking him fishing the next day, to show how the other fishermen respect him as the best in the business. Of course, Peter catches nothing all day. Dejected, he decides to head for shore, and later, Jesus performs the miracle of the "great catch" of fish (Luke 5:1–11). Humbled, Peter says to Jesus, "Go away from me, Lord, for I am a sinful man!" In response to Peter's humility, Jesus rewards Peter by putting him in charge of a new fishing expedition—fishing for men.

One moral of the story is that a realistic self-image is intimately related to God's image. The Bible says as much in the first chapter of Genesis, "God created humankind in his image, in the image of God he created them; male and female he created them" (Genesis 1:27).

If we are indeed created in the image and likeness of God, then each of us bears a "family resemblance" to God. Any attempt to develop a healthy self-perception without taking into account our relationship with God will assuredly fall short. It would be like trying to come to an in-depth under-standing of who we are while ignoring our family of origin. Our ultimate "family of origin" is God.

With that in mind, let me repeat what I said above, with an added clarification: You simply cannot be happy unless you see yourself as you truly are, *and you will never see yourself as you truly are unless you see yourself in relationship with God.*

An inflated sense of self-importance

Sadly, this relationship with God was broken by our first parents. The book of Genesis tells the story of the fall of Adam and Eve. The cause of their fall into sin was not simple disobedience but an inflated sense of self-importance. It was caused by their willingness to entertain the notion that they could be equal to God. In fact, the wily serpent tempted them to eat of the forbidden fruit with these enticing words, "For God knows that when you eat of it your eyes will be opened, and you will be like God, knowing good and evil" (Genesis 3:5).

That's a hard offer to pass up. It's quite affirming—and seductive—to have someone tell you that greatness is within your grasp. Adam and Eve reached for that which belongs only to God, and they ended up alienating themselves from the very God who created them. They responded by hiding from God and by pointing fingers of blame at one another.

We inherit the effects of this bad decision. Tooting your own horn definitely has an adverse effect on everyday relationships and on our relationship with God. The effects include:

An inability
- to listen to authority

- to take criticism or to admit to being wrong
- to ask for help

An increase

- in anxiety and fear
- in self-pity
- in anger and jealousy
- in insecurity

A tendency

- toward legalism
- to criticize others
- toward defensiveness
- toward self-centeredness

A decrease

- in compassion

It's not about you

So an inflated sense of self-importance is no laughing matter. According to Scripture, pride is guaranteed to bring about our downfall. With this caveat in mind, our Christian tradition makes it very clear that the first key to spiritual wellness is to see yourself as you really are.

This is accomplished by following this mantra: *It's not about you.* Your life is not so much about you as it is about what *God is doing* through, with, and in you. We mistakenly think that we are the stars of a show in which God makes an occasional cameo appearance whenever we invite him in. The truth is that God is the writer, producer, director, and star of an epic drama that encompasses all of creation, and he invites each of us to discover our very special and integral role within that drama. Theologian Fr. Robert Barron writes, "Either your life is about Jesus and his mission or it is about you. There is no third option." And it is that first option—a life that is about Jesus and his mission—that is the only sure-fire way to a healthy self-image.

So don't believe the hype

Imagine that someone tells you that you should

- run for office
- write a book
- record a song
- apply for a promotion
- try out for a team
- take a leadership position
- give a speech
- become a fashion model
- audition for a role
- go into business

There's nothing intrinsically wrong with any of these pursuits; in fact, these types of affirmations just may be the encouragement one needs to strive for a worthy goal. It's nice to be told by others that they see potential in you.

Likewise, accomplishments themselves may be very affirming. Imagine if you

- saved your money and finally bought that shiny new car you've had your eye on

- got a promotion and a raise
- had kids who got straight A's on their report cards
- organized and executed a highly successful event
- got a song, article, or book published
- maintained the same physique you had twenty years ago
- moved into a larger home
- were named employee of the month
- received an award

Again, there is nothing wrong with any of the above activities. They are all wonderful accomplishments, and we should indeed take pleasure in our successes. At the same time, temptations come along with these affirmations. An inflated sense of self-importance can take hold of us subtly and gradually. Few people wake up one morning and decide to be arrogant. What happens is that, slowly but surely, we begin to believe the hype about ourselves. We begin to think that we are entitled to the blessings we enjoy. And then, as eventually will happen, someone (or life in general) will treat us in a manner that we feel does not live up to our billing and we feel wronged.

So don't believe the hype. I have no doubt that God must laugh to keep from crying when he observes us patting ourselves on the back for being so amazingly autonomous. Turn a skeptical eye on the inflated sense of self-importance that focuses too much attention on you and not enough attention on other people and God.

Speaking of self-image, it's ironic that so many of us are obsessed with how we appear to the rest of the world, when all we want is to be accepted for who we are. It's no wonder that so many of us choose to live "on the surface," avoiding the inner workings of the soul. Superficiality offers a numbness that often seems preferable to facing the complexities of the inner reality we call the soul. Welcome to the wacky world of self-perception.

Humility—a sure cure for hype

In Christian tradition, authenticity is achieved by practicing humility—something that court jesters reminded their majesties of.

Unfortunately, humility is a virtue that too often gets bad press in our contemporary culture, which tends to view it as a belittling of oneself. However, humility is not about beating ourselves up, belittling ourselves, or even exuding a false modesty. Humility is being able to see ourselves as we really are, and as a result, being able to see others and God as they truly are. Humility is not a denial of our self-worth; it is an affirmation of the inherent worth and dignity of all people and a recognition of our place in that community of people. Humility is the constant recognition of our own worth coupled with the recognition that there is always someone or something greater than ourselves.

Humility creates space for others, whereas a bloated sense of self-importance crowds others—and God—out. When we crowd out others and God from our lives we become accustomed to having control and to following our own will. We lose the ability to listen.

According to Holocaust survivor and author Elie Wiesel, listening plays a central role in our relationship with God. He observes, "In Jewish tradition, the word *listen, listen, listen* is frequently used. The Bible is full of the word *listen*, listen Israel, listen Moses, listen Abraham, listen. The Jew in me says I must listen to others" (from PBS's *First Person Singular*).

It is no coincidence, then, that the primary prayer of the Jewish people, the Shema, begins with the command to listen: "Hear, O Israel: the LORD is our God, the LORD alone" (Deuteronomy 6:4). Jesus himself remarked, "Let anyone with ears to hear listen!" (Mark 4:9). Unfortunately, a swelled head seems to clog the ear canals, preventing us from listening to others and to God. Humility enables us to open our ears, listen to others, and to let go of control.

Humility is not to be confused with timidity, nor is it a lack of self-confidence or meekness. Rather, humility is a bold and confident move away from focusing on the good for oneself and toward seeking the good of the many. An attitude with no pretense improves relationships by decreasing anxiety within those relationships. We get along better with others when we stop comparing ourselves with them. St. Paul said as much in his second letter to the Corinthians: "We do not dare to classify or compare ourselves with some of those who commend themselves. But when they measure themselves by one another, and compare themselves with one another, they do not show good sense" (2 Corinthians 10:12).

An attitude of gratitude

One of the most effective means of learning to see ourselves as we really are and to cultivate a sense of humility is to develop a profound sense of gratitude. The moment we conclude that we are responsible for who we are, what we have done, and what we possess, then we are in big trouble. When we recognize that God is the source of all the blessings in our lives, we respond with an attitude of gratitude.

A profound sense of gratitude reminds us of the source of all good gifts. It reminds us of the responsibility we have to share those blessings with others. This is why Jesus said, "From everyone to whom much has been given, much will ed" (Luke 12:48). Giving thanks to God is not for _nefit, but for our own. God does not need our thanks an_ _ise, but he asks it of us because he knows that when we do so, we will find ourselves in a good place where we can pursue a healthy relationship with him and with one another.

One of the best ways to develop an attitude of gratitude is to practice the Daily Examen, a form of prayer developed by St. Ignatius of Loyola five hundred years ago. The examen is a simple method of reviewing your day in God's presence. The examen prayer, usually accomplished in fifteen to twenty minutes, involves five simple steps:

1. Ask God for light—in order to see your day with God's eyes.
2. Give thanks—for the gift of the day you have just lived.
3. Review the day—guided by the Holy Spirit.
4. Face your shortcomings—humbly acknowledging shortcomings.
5. Look toward the day to come—asking God for help in the day to come.

—Adapted from *A Simple, Life-Changing Prayer*

In particular, step 2, giving thanks, is a needed daily reminder that God is the source of all goodness in our lives. Without a regular practice of giving thanks, we can lull ourselves into patting ourselves on the back for who we are, what we have, and what we've accomplished. In *A Simple, Life-Changing Prayer*, Jim Manney explains that without gratitude we can slip into a "self-centered do-it-yourself attitude—a kind of Ben Franklin-like self-help mentality." Manney goes on to say:

This attitude [is] positively toxic when applied to spiritual matters. It turns the spiritual life into a program of self-improvement. One aspect of the examen that is particularly useful in combating the Ben Franklin temptation is the attitude of thanksgiving and gratitude that permeates the whole exercise. By reminding us that we are not God, the examen shatters the illusion that the world revolves around me.

Step 4 of the examen, acknowledging our shortcomings, keeps us humble. In this step, we attempt to fix what's wrong in our lives by asking pardon for our faults. We are not doing this step as though groveling before a hanging judge and pleading for mercy. Rather, we do it in response to God's invitation to see ourselves as we really are and in light of God's abundant mercy. Manney explains, "If the examen prayer is doing its job, it will bring up painful moments and cause you to look at behavior that's embarrassing. Sometimes you squirm praying the examen, but why would you have it otherwise? Real prayer is about change, and change is never easy."

Humbling ourselves is not easy either. However, it leads to a healthy self-perception. When we see ourselves clearly—recognizing the resemblance we bear to God—we will see ourselves and love ourselves as God sees and loves us. And when we love ourselves in this way, we are capable of following what Jesus said are the greatest commandments: "You shall love the Lord your God with all your heart, and with all your soul, and with all your mind, and with all your strength" and "You shall love your neighbor as yourself" (Mark 12:30–31).

Jesus—humility personified

Jesus is humility personified. Literally. From where did he get his humility? No doubt his earthly parents played a significant role. Joseph, his foster-father, was so humble that he offered "no comment" about his role in raising the Son of God. Not a single word is recorded in Scripture from the mouth of Joseph. Mary did some talking but it was not about herself. She could have strutted through the streets of Nazareth jawing about her special role as the Mother of God. Instead, she turned the spotlight onto God and said, "My soul magnifies the Lord, and my spirit rejoices in God my Savior" (Luke 1:46–47). In fact, in her entire prayer (called the Magnificat, in Luke 1:46–55), Mary used the words *me/my* only five times, while using the words *he/his* fifteen times. In other words, it's all about God.

It's no surprise then, that Jesus epitomizes humility. Unlike Adam and Eve, he did not strive to become like God. Instead, he humbled himself. And, ironically, because of his humility, he is to be praised. Hmm. . . . I think I'll let St. Paul explain this. I can humbly admit that he does it so much better than I ever could!

> Let the same mind be in you that was in Christ Jesus, who, though he was in the form of God, did not regard equality with God as something to be exploited, but emptied himself, taking the form of a slave, being born in human likeness. And being found in human form, he humbled himself and became obedient to the point of death—even death on a cross. Therefore God also highly exalted him and gave him the name that is above every name, so that at the name of Jesus every knee should bend, in heaven and on earth and under the earth, and every tongue should confess that Jesus Christ is Lord, to the glory of God the Father.
>
> —Philippians 2:5–11

KEY 2

Actively Seeking the
Good of Others

What do you have that cannot be taken away?

If you can identify and cultivate the answer to that question, you'll be on your way to spiritual wellness. If you lose sight of it, you'll be opening the door of your soul to a host of unwelcome little gremlins that can mess you up. A great deal of our unhappiness in life can be traced to our fears about losing that which we have: possessions, status, talents, and so on. We become consumed with insecurity, which in turn breeds rivalry and competition. The problem is that we end up constantly comparing ourselves to rivals and competitors, measuring our self-worth by how we stack up next to them. Their gifts, their talents, and their successes threaten our self-worth. The only joy we find is either in our own triumphs or their defeats.

That's why the second key to spiritual wellness—actively seeking the good of others—begins with focusing on what you have that cannot be taken away. This allows you to truly enjoy and contribute to the good fortune of others, content and secure in your own skin. If something cannot be taken away from you, then you have no reason to be insecure. Others will no longer appear to you as rivals, and life will not seem like one big competition. You will be breeding contentment.

I want to make one clarification. We cannot strive for justice without engaging in some comparisons. There are too many examples in life of gross injustices and inequities: some people are benefiting while many others are being unjustly deprived. Such comparisons can lead us to fight for social justice, where we actively seek the good of others by transforming society. The difference is that a comparison for justice's sake can lead us to productively seek the good of others instead of moving us into isolation and apathy. When working for social justice, we are not motivated by ill feelings toward the "haves," but by the desire to see that the "have-nots" receive what God intended.

Why can't I have what they have?

We begin comparing ourselves to others when we are little tots, wondering why someone else's toy is bigger and shinier than ours. As we grow older, it becomes a habit.

- You get dressed up to go out for a night on the town with your friends and then compare outfits, thinking either "Damn, I look good" or "Shoot, why can't I look as good as him/her?"

- You participate in a project at work and compare your performance with coworkers.

- You relax with friends, but start to compare how your stories and jokes are being received compared with those of your friends.

- You drive on the expressway and compare your car to others, and see other drivers as rivals whom we must defeat. (The late comedian George Carlin observed that we tend to think those driving slower than us are "idiots," while those driving faster than us are "maniacs"!)

- You stand on a train platform or wait for a bus and compare your body shape to those standing nearby.

When we do this kind of comparing, we forfeit the ability to determine our own self-worth and hand it over to someone else, measuring ourselves in comparison to their successes or failures and stifling our ability to seek the good of others. The results are not pretty. We can find ourselves

- becoming bitter about the talents, successes, and good fortune of others.

- developing unnecessary rivalries.

- experiencing pleasure at others' difficulties or distress.

- beginning to read false motives into others' behavior.

- becoming more prone to belittling others and engaging in gossip, slander, and backbiting.

- falling prey to prejudice.

- beginning to think of ourselves as "have-nots."

- beginning to think that the good fortune of others somehow diminishes us.

Cain's unfavorable comparison

The unhealthiness of this kind of comparison is shown in one of the most ancient stories of Scripture—the story of Cain and Abel. Both Cain and Abel make an offering to God, but for some unknown reason, Abel's offering is found pleasing to God while Cain's offering is not. One of my religion teachers in grade school attempted to explain this by saying that Abel offered the best of his harvest while Cain offered only rotten leftover scraps. She wanted so badly to make Cain the bad guy and Abel the good guy. But that's not what the story says. No reason is given for why Abel's offering is found pleasing and Cain's is not.

The story reflects one of the harsh realities of life: @#%& happens! Bad things indeed do happen to good people. Cain doesn't like this. He compares himself to his brother Abel, and he doesn't like what he sees about himself or his brother. Things go downhill from there. By comparing himself to his brother, Cain comes to disdain Abel; although in reality, Cain's disdain is for himself. God reaches out to Cain, asking him why he is so angry and dejected and warning him that "sin is lurking at the door" (Genesis 3:7). Sadly, Cain does not respond to God's voice within. Rather, he continues to cultivate misery by comparing himself to Abel, thus measuring his own self-worth against something outside of himself. As a result, Cain frets about what may be taken away from him instead of accepting God's invitation to recognize what cannot be taken away from him—namely, his relationship with God.

This story also illustrates another truism about the danger of comparing ourselves to others: We tend to compare ourselves to those who are closest to us and most similar to us. Think about it. If you participate in a 5-kilometer or 10-kilometer race, you usually don't compare yourself with the front runners (unless you are of Olympic caliber). Rather, you compare yourself to those directly ahead of you, those who are running even with you, and those who are directly behind you.

I recall one time, as I was entering the home stretch of a 5-K run, I looked up and saw a ten-year-old kid about an eighth of a mile ahead of me. I wasn't about to let this little punk beat me. Tired as I was, I dug down deep to find some extra energy and began to close the gap as the finish line came into view. Just as I was about to overtake him, he put on an amazing burst of youthful speed, leaving me in the dust. I'm sure he was determined not to be defeated by a middle-aged man. I finished the run in good time for someone my age, but I couldn't let go of a sense of having been defeated. By comparing myself with this young athlete, I had inadvertently handed over to him the power to determine my self-worth. I took no joy in his success and felt only agitation at what I perceived to be my own failure.

In a no-win situation, change the rules of the game

This cycle of comparison creates a no-win scenario. There are people all around us who have bigger homes, better body shapes, more money, better jobs, seemingly happier families, fancier cars, and better (or more) hair than we do. Seeking the good of others is difficult when comparisons make us more aware of our own shortcomings. We need to change the rules of the game because we'll lose the game we are playing right now.

What do I mean about a no-win scenario and changing the rules of the game? An example comes from the movie *Star Trek*. Every cadet at Star Fleet Academy undergoes an intense test of character in a no-win scenario called the *Kobayashi Maru* test. In this simulation, the cadet leads a crew into enemy territory to rescue a civilian ship named the *Kobayashi Maru* that has come under attack by the evil Klingons. The cadet can either go forward with the rescue attempt and risk intergalactic war, or abandon the attempt and leave the crew of the *Kobayashi Maru* to face certain death. Further complicating the matter, once the cadet leads his crew into enemy territory, they find themselves surrounded and under attack with no way out—a true no-win scenario. The only person to ever defeat the no-win scenario was young James T. Kirk, who later goes on to command the U.S.S. *Enterprise.* How did he win at a no-win scenario? He changed the rules of the game! Before participating in the test, Kirk reprogrammed the simulator's computer to alter the possible outcomes. He created a new game.

Luckily for us Christians, we follow someone who has changed the rules of the game, someone who offers us a new reality and who does not believe in a no-win scenario. Jesus Christ defeated the no-win scenario and invites us to enter into a new reality—the kingdom of God—in which we can play according to a whole new set of rules. In this reality, we no longer need to compare ourselves to those who

- are richer than us, because it is blessed to be poor.
- seem happier than us, because it is blessed to mourn.
- seem mightier than us, because it is blessed to be meek.
- get away with doing wrong, because it is blessed to hunger and thirst for righteousness.
- crush their opponents, because it is blessed to show mercy.
- triumph by force, because it is blessed to be a peacemaker.

- seem to go through life unscathed, because it is blessed
  to be persecuted for the sake of righteousness.

Jesus' new rules create a new reality called the kingdom of
God, where we find true happiness because one thing cannot
be taken away from us—the reign of God in our hearts.
Instead of feeling resentful, angry, or sad when we're hungry
and persecuted, Jesus says that we are blessed. Really? I mean,
really? What is so darn blessed about being poor, mourning,
or being persecuted? In and of themselves, nothing. Jesus is
teaching us to recognize that we can always still find contentment in knowing that we are blessed in the eyes of
God—something that cannot be taken away from us.

Why St. Paul found contentment in affliction

Those followers of Jesus who have done very well playing by
the "new rules" of Jesus' Beatitudes are called *saints*. One of
the best examples of someone who successfully "put on" the
mind of Jesus was St. Paul. He seems to have mastered the art
of not comparing himself to others. Instead, he focused his
attention on that which could not be taken away from him,
namely, his relationship with Jesus Christ.

> Who will separate us from the love of Christ? Will hard-
> ship or distress, or persecution, or famine, or nakedness,
> or peril, or sword? . . . No, in all these things we are
> more than conquerors through him who loved us. For
> I am convinced that neither death, nor life, nor angels,
> nor rulers, nor things present, nor things to come, nor
> powers, nor height, nor depth, nor anything else in all
> creation, will be able to separate us from the love of God
> in Christ Jesus our Lord.
>
> —Romans 8:35–39

How's that for certainty? Paul mentions many things that we may think threaten our well-being. Then he identifies the key to conquering such fears: focusing on the intimate and enduring relationship that God offers us through his Son, Christ Jesus our Lord—something that cannot be taken away. Paul's recognition of this indissoluble relationship permitted him to actively seek the good of others, finding contentment even when he was faced with suffering and cruel hardships that would make most of us shrivel.

> We are afflicted in every way, but not crushed; perplexed, but not driven to despair; persecuted, but not forsaken; struck down, but not destroyed; always carrying in the body the death of Jesus, so that the life of Jesus may also be made visible in our bodies. . . . So we do not lose heart. Even though our outer nature is wasting away, our inner nature is being renewed day by day. For this slight momentary affliction is preparing us for an eternal weight of glory beyond all measure, because we look not at what can be seen but at what cannot be seen; for what can be seen is temporary, but what cannot be seen is eternal.
>
> —2 Corinthians 4:8–10, 16–18

Paul could easily have slipped into pretty serious depression by comparing his life of hardships to others. Remember, this was a man who experienced temporary blindness, a sudden change of career, stoning, taunts, imprisonments, shipwrecks, and physical ailments. Despite all of these, he continued to rejoice. Why? Because he had come to the realization that the most valuable thing to him—his relationship with God in Christ Jesus—could not be taken away from him. In fact, it was at a time when Paul was feeling sorry for himself that he came to this realization. One time when he was praying about his afflictions, he heard God say, "My grace is sufficient for you" (2 Corinthians 12:9). And grace is nothing other than a living, breathing relationship with God—a relationship that cannot be taken away.

Grace

Saints who learned to play by new rules

This same realization has fueled the lives of countless saints throughout the ages. St. Ignatius of Loyola, who firmly believed in doing spiritual exercises to strengthen spiritual muscles, composed the following prayer, echoing St. Paul's understanding of grace.

> Take, Lord, and receive all my liberty,
> my memory, my understanding, and my entire will,
> all I have and call my own.
>
> You have given all to me.
> To you, Lord, I return it.
>
> Everything is yours; do with it what you will.
> Give me only your love and your grace.
> That is enough for me.

Ignatius is saying, "Go ahead and take away all those things that can be taken away from me, but give me that which cannot be taken away—your relationship (grace) with me."

St. Francis of Assisi also abided by Jesus' new rules, finding happiness in that which cannot be taken away.

> O Divine Master, grant that I may not so much seek
> to be consoled as to console;
> to be understood as to understand;
> to be loved as to love.

For it is in giving that we receive;
it is in pardoning that we are pardoned;
and it is in dying that we are born to eternal life.

Blessed Mother Teresa of Calcutta is also a great example
of someone who abided by Jesus' new rules. Her steadfast
embrace of that which cannot be taken away enabled her to
actively seek the good of others and to abide by the following
words, which we can all take to heart.

People are often unreasonable, illogical and
    self-centered;
forgive them anyway.

If you are kind, people may accuse you of selfish,
    ulterior motives;
be kind anyway.

If you are successful, you will win some false friends and
    some true enemies;
succeed anyway.

If you are honest and frank, people may cheat you;
be honest and frank anyway.

What you spend years building, someone could destroy
    overnight;
build anyway.

If you find serenity and happiness, they may be jealous;
be happy anyway.

The good you do today, people will often forget
    tomorrow;
do good anyway.

Give the world the best you have, and it may never be
   enough;
give the world the best you've got anyway.

You see, in the final analysis, it is between you and your
   God;
it was never between you and them anyway.

Turn competition to your advantage

How is it possible to seek the good of others in a world filled
with so much competition? The solution is not to avoid competition but to engage in it for the right reasons. If we focus
our attention on that which cannot be taken away from us,
we can compare ourselves to others as a means of growing
as a person. After "losing" to a ten-year-old in a 5-K run, I
have learned to watch runners who appear to be my same age
and weight, and who appear to be running at a pace close to
mine. By comparing myself to them, I can judge how my own
pace is going. I can compete with them but not set them up
as rivals. As a result, my self-worth isn't tied up with beating
them. I am a child of God and that God delights in me for no
other reason than the fact that he created me. When I know
this, I can enjoy competition simply because I love the sport
and not because I have to win. We learn to value our competitors, seeing them not as rivals but as partners in seeking
excellence.

Many athletes and teachers maintain that the best way
to grow in a skill is to practice with or against someone
who is better than you. Some years ago, when I was working
in parish ministry, I made a regular habit of attending the
open gym at the parish on Saturday mornings. A group of
young African-American men from the nearby Altgeld Gar-
dens housing project would come over to play basketball. I'm

sure they wondered who this old white guy was trying to keep up with them, but I was determined to play every week even though I was supremely outclassed. I could enjoy playing the game because I had no delusions that I was the best. I also developed my skills and endurance.

The payoff is seeking the good of others

Mark? When we have no fear of losing that which cannot be taken away from us, *we become capable of actively seeking the good of others*. We usually want the best for our loved ones: spouses, parents, children, siblings, close friends. We see them—especially our family—as an extension of ourselves. But we do not have to confine our charitable attitudes to that inner circle. We need to expand that circle and love an ever expanding population, until we have mastered the technique of seeing every human being as another self and loving them accordingly.

This doesn't mean that we have to develop feelings of affection for everyone we meet. Actively seeking the good of others is something that we can achieve with a sense of detachment. This kind of love is called "disinterested" love. It doesn't sound very loving to be *disinterested*, but that's not what the term means. Disinterested love is love that has no regard for oneself. Is it possible to love others without seeking to be loved in return? Yes, but only when one knows at the very core of his or her being, that he or she is already loved by God.

To love without strings attached is how God loves. It's the kind of love that we're referring to when we say that "God is love." This is a love that wants what is best for others based on the recognition that they, like us, are made in the image and likeness of God. This enables us to live according to the

Golden Rule, doing unto others as we would have done unto ourselves, namely because others are "another self."

Loving with Ignatian indifference

In the Ignatian tradition, this kind of disinterested love is known as "Ignatian indifference." St. Ignatius of Loyola, the founder of the Jesuits, taught that when we recognize that our reason for living is to be in intimate communion with God, we can become "indifferent" to everything else. That doesn't mean being apathetic or uncaring, but indifferent in the sense of being detached from created things. We learn to love others not as an end in itself but as a means to an end—as a way of participating in the Divine Life. When we learn to live with "Ignatian indifference," loving others with a disinterested love, we become capable of

- maintaining our spiritual and emotional balance
- avoiding inordinate attachments on people or things
- attaching ourselves to God who is holy
- becoming holy ourselves
- resisting envy
- enjoying inner freedom
- making decisions based solely on what will enable us to better love God and others
- adopting a posture of readiness in order to more clearly see God's will in our lives

St. Ignatius says that this attitude of indifference permits us to accept whatever comes, whether that is

- to be rich or poor

- to be clever or dull
- to be handsome or ugly
- to be strong or weak
- to be attractive or repulsive
- to be educated or illiterate
- to be healthy or sick
- to be active or jobless
- to be considered or forgotten
- to be loved or ignored
- to be successful or to be a failure
- to be honored or despised
- to be rewarded or passed over
- to be popular or unknown
- to have friends or to be lonely
- to live long or to die young

Wanting what you've got

In Christian tradition, this attitude of detachment is known as "poverty," a concept all too often misunderstood even by Christians themselves. To practice poverty is not to walk around in rags with your stomach grumbling for food. It is detachment from material goods. Sheryl Crow sang about it in her song, "Soak up the Sun"—"It's not having what you want; it's wanting what you've got." This spirit of poverty is not restricted to nuns and monks. The truth is, nuns and monks make a sacred vow to live lives of poverty in order to remind the rest of us that poverty is one of the keys to spiritual wellness. It is indeed blessed to be poor, even if that poverty is in spirit only. If you live with a spirit of poverty (detachment, disinterested love), then you will find yourself taking joy in the success of others and actively seeking their good. This is the second key of spiritual wellness.

KEY 3

Thinking Before
Acting

Is that your final answer?

That's the question asked of every contestant on the television quiz show *Who Wants to Be a Millionaire?* Four answers are offered for each question. As the questions get harder, contestants use "lifelines" for help, ranging from polling the audience to actually phoning a friend for help. There is a dramatic pause while the contestant thinks about it, and then announces his or her answer. The emcee then says, "Is that your final answer?" In other words, "Have you thoroughly thought through your options and the consequences?"

This is the third key to spiritual wellness: *thinking before acting*. Spirituality is not mindlessness. It is the synergy of heart and mind working together. We are taught to love God with our whole heart, soul, *mind*, and strength. We do not leave our minds at the door when it comes to spirituality. Unfortunately, many people consider thinking to be

31

burdensome. We are encouraged to "just do it," especially if it feels good. Acting without thinking is a sure path to a spirituality that is crippled by only having one leg to stand on.

Three good reasons to think before you act

Acting without thinking often feels good because it provides us with a sense of certainty and control. We just follow our impulses and let loose. This sense of immediate gratification was epitomized in the 1976 film *Network* in which a deranged television anchorman, played by Peter Finch, encouraged people to open their windows and yell, "I'm mad as hell and I'm not going to take this anymore!" Immediately, people all over the country opened their windows and released all their rage. Why not? It feels good to let loose without thinking.

But there are three big problems when we let loose without thinking:

- Our response happens too quickly.
- Our response is usually too excessive.
- The effects of our response linger for too long.

Emotions and reason are intimately connected. The emotion of anger actually begins with thinking. We react angrily because our mind has concluded that we have been wronged. Our thinking awakens emotions that march into battle without a battle plan.

Strong emotions such as anger lack judgment. Left alone, anger is reactive and unreflective, and its ultimate goal is the destruction of the object or person who has aroused it. This is why anger management strategies almost always include taking a few deep breaths and counting to ten before responding. We need to allow enough time for the brain to ask the emotions, "Is that your final answer?" A ten-second time-out can provide the brain with just the time it needs to attach a leash to the emotions and say, "Whoa there, big guy. Let's work together on this!"

In the air without visible means of support

We admire people who shoot first and ask questions later because they seem to embody the quality that we wish we possessed: certainty. We all would like to stand on solid ground in a world that is black and white. That's why religious fundamentalism is so attractive to many spiritual seekers; it offers a false sense of certainty. Instead, we have to learn to be comfortable with ambiguity and doubt.

Fr. Richard Rohr illustrates this point with a thought experiment. You have a stone table, and next to the table is a flying carpet. The table is solid; its legs are strong. The Lord says, "Come," so you climb onto the solid table. But the Lord points to the carpet and says, "No, over here." You're afraid; the carpet is floating without support. The Lord says he will sustain you, so you get on the carpet. The wind tosses you around; you're afraid again. Then the Lord starts pulling threads out of the carpet! You jump onto the solid table, but the Lord invites you to get on the carpet. Rohr continues:

> You meekly get back on the carpet. Once again you feel the excitement. Once again you feel the wind. Once again you look around and—wouldn't you know it? The Lord's at it again, pulling out the threads. So there you are. The carpet is getting threadbare. The wind is getting gusty. The stone table looks so secure. He reassures you, "That's not where it's at. This is where life is. I will be your joy. I will be your hope. I will be your fullness." "Okay, Lord," you say. And as the time goes on, you see

the Lord continuing to pull out the threads until finally there is nothing left but him. And that's exactly what God wanted you to see. That's exactly what you needed to experience for yourself. It was not the power of the carpet that sustained you; it was the power of the Lord. (from *The Great Themes of Scripture: Old Testament*)

This is how life often feels—as though we are afloat on a flimsy flying carpet, buffeted by the winds, and God seems to be pulling the threads out from under us! Certainty eludes us just when we feel we need it most. We crave it. We seek it. Without it we're afraid.

We're in trouble, because we have confused *certainty* with *truth*. In real life, certainty is a myth. In his book *The Myth of Certainty*, Daniel Taylor explains that "the ruling methodology for reaching truth in much of the secular culture, also influential in some religious spheres, reflects the dominance of the scientific model. Essentially, one amasses evidence . . . until one reaches something very like certainty, until one has *proof*." This is very appealing to us. Taylor goes on:

Make no mistake; this approach to truth is enormously powerful and attractive. Our appetite for certainty has only grown in our troubled century. The further away it is, the more desirable it seems. Who would not want this kind of certainty if it were available? As insecurity threatens on so many fronts, the man who offers a guarantee with faith will attract a large and devoted following. He will appear, not without reason, as a man of conviction, a prophet, a defender of the faith against the forces of evil.

The truth is that doubt and faith go hand in hand for finite creatures such as us. We can begin with this nugget of wisdom from poet Khalil Gibran, who reminds us that "doubt is a pain too lonely to know that faith is his twin brother." For this reason, pausing to think before acting enables doubt and faith, as well as our thinking and emotions, to enter into a dialogue. Ten seconds of uncertainty can give us just the time we need to respond to a situation in a manner that we—and those on the receiving end of our response—can live with.

What to do when you are under pressure

Many times circumstances don't allow us the luxury of careful deliberation. Here are some tips for doing discernment under fire.

Stop. Take a few moments, count to ten, and breathe deeply. This can help get your emotions in check.

Speak clearly. Once you have your emotions in check and your thinking is jump-started, express yourself without attacking the other person verbally. Clearly and assertively state your feelings and concerns.

Get active. Some kind of physical activity will stimulate various chemicals in the brain that can calm you down and help you to think more clearly.

Slow the game down. Consider your words carefully so that you don't say something you'll later regret. Slow down the "pace of the game" to allow cooler heads to prevail.

Seek a solution. Allow your thinking to move from focusing on what has upset you to seeking a resolution.

Speak for yourself. Express yourself using "I" statements. Describe how you feel. Don't point fingers and throw fuel on the fire. Don't make accusations that begin with "you."

Use humor. Everyone involved will be able to think more clearly if the mood is lightened.

Use a lifeline! Like the contestants on *Who Wants to Be a Millionaire?*, seek help from various lifelines. In some situations, we simply must admit that we aren't capable of thinking clearly. When this happens, invite another person to step in to help you and others involved think before acting.

Making good decisions

Thinking that puts the brain and the heart in dialogue is known as *discernment*. It's a vital part of a healthy spirituality. St. Ignatius of Loyola used the word *discernment* to describe the process of thinking before acting. Discernment seeks to align our will with the will of God so that we can learn what God is calling us to do and become. Every choice we make, no matter how small, is an opportunity to get in touch with our spiritual life, as long as we bring thinking and feeling into dialogue.

"For Christians, thinking is a part of believing," writes Robert Louis Wilken in *The Spirit of Early Christian Thought*. What kind of thinking should precede action? Here are three questions to ask yourself to stimulate your thinking before swinging into action.

"What am I choosing to do?" If the action is intrinsically evil, the act as a whole is wrong no matter how good the intention is. Of critical importance here is identifying the consequences of your action.

"Why am I choosing this action?" In other words, identify your true intentions. A good intention does not justify an evil action. The end does not justify the means.

"When, how, and where am I performing
Circumstances play a role in determining th
an action. The circumstances surrounding a
have a profound influence on the extent to
action can be considered moral or not.

Here are some strategies for incorporating reflection or discernment into your decision-making process.

- Talk to someone you respect.
- Find some solitude.
- Start with what you know.
- Tell God what you desire and what you fear.
- Let God speak to you.
- Know that God has a plan for you and pray to follow his will.
- Be patient.
- Prayerfully commit to your decision.
- Check out the fruits of your decision.

Asking for help
doesn't mean you're weak

One of the reasons that we too often forgo thinking before acting is because we believe it makes us look weak—particularly if we have to use a "lifeline." This is especially true of men like me, who can barely stand the thought of stopping the car to ask for directions when we are hopelessly lost. We think that pausing to ask for help somehow undermines our own sense of authority and certainty. This way of thinking pervades our whole culture. American society in general is suspicious of any kind of authority outside of our own.

One of the biggest proponents of this way of thinking is television host Oprah Winfrey. She has asserted "you are your own best authority" in her efforts to impart a vague brand of spirituality to her audiences. Echoing the message of author Eckhart Tolle, Winfrey has emphasized that spirituality has nothing to do with doctrine—teachings that are set forth by an authority outside of ourselves. This appeals to the many people who are absolutely certain that their voice is the sole voice of authority, and that it's not necessary to listen to any-one else's wisdom. At the same time many people today are all too happy to impose their own brand of authority on oth-ers through violence and force. The truth is that it's wise to reach out and use the "lifelines" in our lives—those other voices (including voices of authority) that can help us think straight when our own thinking has been overthrown by our emotions.

To acknowledge a voice of authority other than our own is an act of humility. It is a way of saying, "I do not have all of the answers. I may have strong feelings and opinions, but I am willing to consider another viewpoint before I act." Ultimately, this is what a conscience provides. Our conscience acts as a recording device, capturing the voices of those people whose wisdom we are willing to consider and embrace as our own. When faced with a decision, even under fire, we can pause to think before we act, consulting the voices within us that can guide us to act in a way that we won't regret.

The ABCDEs of prudent thinking

When you get down to it, this whole process of thinking before acting is as easy as ABC and D . . . well, actually ABCD and E. ABCDE—here's what I'm talking about.

A gent Provocateur. This term describes a person who is hired to covertly entice or provoke someone to act illegally or at least rashly. This is where the thinking-before-acting trouble begins: life provokes us. Life is full of "agent provocateurs." It could be as simple as someone looking at you the wrong way or cutting in front of you on the expressway. It could be as dramatic as someone betraying you. Either way, you have been slapped across the face with a pair of white gloves and challenged to a duel.

B elief Filter. Your reaction to the provocation is determined by your beliefs. Your belief filter says you've been wronged. The thinking that takes place here is short-lived . . . more like a triage than an operating room. Almost immediately your emotions step in and say, "OK, thanks for the diagnosis . . . We'll take it from here." In the long run we can work to alter our belief system so that we don't interpret everything as a threat. We can change the rules of the game. This is where we need the gospel of Jesus to transform our thinking so that our belief filter is not weighed down by fears.

C onsequent Emotions. The time it takes to get from A to B to C can be measured in nanoseconds. As quickly as your thinking determines that you've been wronged, your emotions snap to attention ready to respond. If you let the process continue on its own, you typically end up doing or saying something you later regret, wondering, "I don't know what got into me!" What you need to do is throw a road block up so that your consequent emotions do not have the final say in the situation. That brings us to D.

Delay for Deliberation. You've gone from thinking to feeling in a split second, leaving your brains behind. Now you need to deliberately pause and reattach the wiring to your brain that the emotions pulled loose in their hurry to charge into battle. It doesn't take long—about ten seconds or so—but in the heat of the moment, that can feel like an eternity. It's important to know that this restraint is not submission. Patience is sorely needed here in order to allow the thinking to catch up to the emotions and respond in a constructive manner. Don't underestimate the power of humor to diffuse the situation at this point, allowing space for everyone's emotions to cool their jets and for their thinking to get revved up. Strong negative emotions narrow our vision while humor expands vision.

Eventual Response. Having rebooted your brain and reunited thinking and feeling, you are now capable of a response that is measured and under control—one that enables you to move forward spiritually integrated. Without this integration, you risk alienating yourself from others. You also risk creating disharmony within yourself, because you recognize that you have not acted in a manner worthy of someone created in the image and likeness of a God who is slow to anger. The integration of the mind and the heart makes it possible for you to experience peace because it aligns your will more closely with God's will, so that his will may be done on earth as it is in heaven.

Thinking is not without its own faults. Too much thinking can paralyze us into inaction. The emotions, which need to be curbed by thinking, also possess the strength to pull up the anchor that thinking would be all too happy to leave in place.

While thinking often needs to say "Whoa!" to the emotions, the emotions sometimes need to say "Giddy-up!" to thinking.

The bright side of anger

Likewise, anger is not always a bad thing. Anger is at the heart of combating injustice. It angers us (or at least it should) to see people who are denied basic resources to sustain their human dignity. When we witness such injustices, our anger is awakened. However, the efforts to right these wrongs cannot be driven by anger, even if anger serves as the catalyst for such efforts. In the long run, we come to the realization that justice belongs to God and that we simply have a role to play in God's larger agenda.

We find it reassuring to see that our God is portrayed on more than one occasion in Scripture as displaying anger. For some people this fact is a contradiction. How can a God who is love display anger? It's important to note that God's anger is not random and impulsive but is always directed at evil. God reminds us over and over again that we grow when we worship something greater than ourselves, and we diminish when we worship something lesser than ourselves. It angers God to see his children engage in actions that diminish them. Our God is passionate and his anger is to be feared. However, the very people who often felt the brunt of God's anger, the Chosen People, were the same people who described God as being "slow to anger." Would you prefer a passion-less God who was indifferent to our comings and goings?

When I was a kid, I recognized my dad's great love for us, his children, when I saw him get really angry one time. My brothers and I were playing whiffle ball on a street a few blocks from home. An elderly woman who lived on the street was annoyed at our presence and called the police. One of us ran to get Dad and he quickly came to see what was going on. The police came and saw a group of seven or eight boys playing with a plastic bat and ball. They told the lady to calm down, and they left. But the woman continued yelling and screaming at us, accusing us of all kinds of mischief. Finally, when she falsely accused us of breaking windows in her apartment, Dad had had enough. He waved a finger in her face and shouted, "That's a G-damn lie and you know it!" We had never heard Dad curse before. The one and only time that we saw our dad angry enough to curse was to protect the children he loved. No doubt, Dad went to confession at the next possible opportunity to ask forgiveness for taking the Lord's name in vain. However, this episode revealed to me just how much my dad loved us and to what lengths he would go to protect us. That's what God's anger is all about.

Scripture also shows that God thinks before acting. One of the most interesting examples of this is found in Exodus 32. God reacts angrily to the fact that his Chosen People have abandoned him in favor of worshipping a golden calf, knowing that his people were now worshipping something that would diminish them. God angrily announces that he will unleash his wrath on his people. But Moses engages God in a conversation, pleading with him to spare his people. God reconsiders his plan. He withholds his wrath and spares his people. This story is not intended to teach us that we can change God's mind; rather, we see God modeling for us the kind of behavior he wants us to follow, since we are made in his image and likeness. We are called to follow his example and think before acting, lest we do something that we will regret. God allowed Moses to act as his "lifeline." Before offering his "final answer," God "listened" to the reasoning of Moses.

Jesus shares his Father's passion. On more than one occasion, Jesus expresses anger, none more obvious than the story of the cleansing of the temple, in which Jesus formed a whip of cords and overturned the money changers' tables (John 2:13–22). If that's not anger, I don't know what is. But Jesus' actions are well thought out, not impulsive. Jesus knew that all of his actions were being closely scrutinized and he used his actions as signs to point to the in-breaking of the kingdom of God.

Cleansing the temple was not about ridding the temple of unscrupulous merchants who should be doing their business elsewhere. No, these merchants were an integral part of the temple sacrificial system, providing animals needed for sacrifices as a way of worshipping God. Jesus' actions signify the end of an era. By cleansing the temple of the money changers, Jesus is proclaiming the end of one form of sacrificial worship and announcing the birth of a new kind of worship, in which he himself was the sacrificial Lamb. Jesus' anger was directed at all the people of Israel who seem to have missed the point: "I desire steadfast love and not sacrifice, the knowledge of God rather than burnt offerings" (Hosea 6:6).

Wear the helmet of salvation

Jesus' cleansing of the temple reminds us that we are called to be like God, who is "slow to anger" and "abounding in steadfast love" (Psalm 145:8). By thinking before we act, we can make sure that our actions are directed toward achieving a goal that is part of God's agenda, not our own. Righteous anger furthers the goal of achieving justice; whereas unrighteous anger can destroy everything in its path in order to achieve an immediate feeling of control and certainty.

Jesus emphasized the role of thinking before acting when he asked, "What king, going out to wage war against another king, will not sit down first and consider whether he is able with ten thousand to oppose the one who comes against him with twenty thousand?" (Luke 14:31). Thinking helps us to choose our battles wisely, ensuring that we do not march into battle without the proper equipment.

Among the many pieces of armor that St. Paul encourages us to wear is the "helmet of salvation" (Ephesians 6:17). Of course, a helmet protects the head, the place where thinking occurs.

Don't leave home without it.

KEY 4

Holding on Loosely

What's your security blanket?

For young children security blankets and other such comfort objects are healthy things. They are "transitional objects"
to ease the trauma of separating from their mothers. For me,
it was my teddy bear, Ya-Ya. For my older brother Tom, it was
his Mr. Magoo doll. For my little sister Anne, it was her doll,
Mrs. Beasely. For my son, Mike, it was his Stay-Puffed Marsh-
mallow plush toy. Let's face it; separating from mommy can
be a frightening experience. However, we all must eventually
cut the apron strings and leave our security blankets behind.
At some point, I outgrew Ya-Ya.

Unfortunately, we tend to replace these plush toys with
more sophisticated security blankets, not to ease the anxiety of
our separation from our mothers, but to ease our separation
from God. Spiritually, we tend to live our lives like little E.T.,
the extraterrestrial being in the famous Stephen Spielberg
film. E.T. experienced separation anxiety when his mother
ship left him behind on earth. Separated from God, we fill

the void with other possessions—our adult security blankets—not realizing that God is nearer to us than we are to ourselves. The human condition has created the illusion that we are separated from God and that we must work to bridge the gap. In truth, the key to spiritual wellness is the removal of influences that perpetuate this illusion and the recognition of the nearness of God.

And so to overcome our anxiety we acquire things. We amass possessions. Not so much because we like the possessions themselves, but because we like the *feeling* of possessing. It provides us with a sense of control—something that will give us the illusion of security and, at least for a while, mask the fear and want that haunt us deep within. Our adult security blankets are like an ever-widening moat that we dig around ourselves to keep the future at bay. We are a society of hoarders, clinging to our possessions because we fear a future in which our happiness, security, and comfort are uncertain.

We are living in a material world

Before we go any further, let's be clear that possessions are not bad. I am not about to rant against materialism. In fact, to do so would be anti-Christian. Pop singer Madonna wasn't entirely wrong when she sang, years ago, "We are living in a material world and I am a material girl." God wants us to enjoy his material creation. The first creation story in the book of Genesis says that the created world is good but that there is a limit.

God put a lot of time and effort into creating the material world, and I'm sure he'd be very upset if we turned our noses up at it. Imagine being invited to someone's home as a special dinner guest. Upon being welcomed to their table that is lavishly filled with delights, you say, "No thanks, I'll just have a glass of water and a pretzel." To refuse to partake in such a

meal would be an insult to the host. Compared to o
gions, Christianity has a soft spot for the material wo

Of all Christian denominations, Catholicism is by far
the most materialistic. At the heart of Catholic spirituality
are the sacraments, which employ materials from God's creation—water, oil, fire, cloth, bread, wine—as channels of
God's grace. Despite the many ascetics over the centuries who
have contributed to the impression that Catholicism con-
demns material goods, Catholicism is actually quite earthy. So
much so that St. Ignatius of Loyola insisted that God could
be found in all things.

The key to spiritual wellness is not to condemn materialism and to avoid it at all costs. Rather, we are called to enjoy
God's creation, while also recognizing that these very same
material goods are only representative of the deeper joy that
comes from encountering the One who created them in the
first place. Enjoying the good of this world is part of a healthy
spirituality. What harms our soul is trying to satisfy our need
and desire for God with material goods and possessions. The
key to a healthy spirituality is *to hold on loosely to the things of
this world*, recognizing that we need to hold on tightly to that
which is unseen.

How do we know if we are holding on too tightly to
material possessions? Here are four questions to ask yourself.

- How much of my time and energy is focused on my
  wealth and possessions?

- To what extent am I comparing myself to others in
  terms of wealth and possessions?

- How painful is it for me to let go of my wealth and possessions to share with others?

- Where and how am I spending my money?

After reflecting on your answers to these questions, you will have a better idea of the condition of your soul and the actions you might need to take to find more balance.

Detecting lifestyle inflation

Problems with possessions and money are subtle. Few of us set out to become materialistic. It just has a way of happening to us. Below are four significant ways in which our lives sometimes just "get away" from us, resulting in what we can call "lifestyle inflation." This is the reality that no matter how much our income increases, our spending always seems to match or exceed it.

The windfall effect

Let's face it, whenever we come into some kind of money, whether from a pay raise, a new job, a bonus, or winning the lottery, we usually inflate our lifestyle to fit. Things that were once just a bit out of our reach can now be obtained, and so we obtain them, not realizing that we will eventually need another infusion of money to reach the next level of the lifestyle ladder.

The ripple effect

This happens when we have a "fling" and purchase something that is outside of our usual price range. We may convince ourselves that it is a once-in-a-lifetime purchase. But the purchase usually has a ripple effect, meaning that there are other related costs. A more expensive car brings higher insurance rates. A more expensive dress is going to need a more expensive pair of shoes and a handbag to go along.

The grass is greener effect

Our tendency to compare ourselves to others is hard enough to resist when the greatest temptation is to look out the window at our neighbor's lawn. However, with today's social media and relentless marketing, it's as if we have countless next-door neighbors and "lawns" to see, making us feel that we are missing something. When we see pictures, posts, and updates of vacations, new cars, and new homes, it's hard not to compare and want what others have.

The pampering effect

We may occasionally decide to treat ourselves to a luxury as a way of pampering ourselves or rewarding ourselves. Perhaps a trip to the spa after a busy week at work. Perhaps that fantasy baseball camp we always dreamed of. The problem begins when we make such pampering a regular feature in our lives. The spa becomes a weekly occurrence. The fantasy baseball camp becomes an annual pilgrimage. There's nothing inherently wrong with either activity, except that lifestyle inflation makes it just a little bit harder to recognize the stranger who stands at our gate. This is precisely what Jesus warns us about in the parable of the rich man who did not recognize the poor beggar, Lazarus, at his gate (Luke 16:19–31). The rich man suffered separation from God (hell) not because he directly hurt Lazarus, but precisely because he didn't take note of him.

Getting off the merry-go-round

How do we break out of this cycle of holding on too tightly to material goods and the discontentment that accompanies it? The solution is not to condemn all materialism or consumerism. That's just not realistic nor is it what God expects of us. The key to getting off of this materialistic merry-go-round is to outsmart it. Here are some ways to learn how to hold on loosely to your material possessions.

Step back and observe your patterns of behavior, taking notice of the reasons and occasions that drive you to acquire in the first place. Before long, you'll realize that your shopping sprees are closely tied to certain emotions that surface as the result of various life experiences.

Recognize that inner happiness cannot be achieved by external realities. Recognize that the connection between possessions and happiness is an illusion.

Understand the differences between healthy self-interest (acquiring possessions out of the obligation you have to yourself and those you're responsible for), a healthy drive to achieve (ambition), and an *un*healthy desire to possess that competes with the self-interest and ambition of others.

Ask yourself *why* you are about to buy something and whether you really need it. Often, just by asking yourself this question, you will recognize what it was that triggered your desire to acquire in the first place.

Distinguish between the *emotional* value of a possession and its *functional* value. When you are able to focus on its functional value, you no longer associate possessions with your happiness but instead, simply enjoy them as one of life's luxuries that you're blessed to have. No longer will you view possessions as the roots of your being but you will see them simply as ornaments that adorn the branches of your life.

Shift from acquiring possessions to *engaging in experiences* as a means to feel a sense of enjoyment and contentment.

The joy of an experience greatly outlasts the fleeting happiness of acquiring a possession. Time spent with friends, going for a walk or bike ride, watching a good movie, going dancing, going to a concert—all of these experiences can reach a much deeper part of our being than acquiring a possession can, and their effects linger much longer than a new car smell does.

The antidote to consumerism: generosity and detachment

All of the above steps, while helpful, are still only treating the symptoms of the problems we encounter when we allow ourselves to be consumed by consumerism. The real antidote is an attitude that can be summed up in two words: *generosity* and *detachment*. We don't overcome consumerism by plunging ourselves into poverty, but by learning how to detach from our possessions. As we learn how to hold on to them more loosely, we will share them more freely and generously. In the Gospels, Jesus does not tell rich people that they need to become poor; rather, that they need to be generous in giving of their riches to others.

The truth is that people who are poor can still be materialistic and possessive. However, it is impossible to be simultaneously generous and selfish. Many people find that generosity and detachment are enriched and strengthened through regular planned giving to charities. The measure of generosity is not the quantity of giving but the spirit of giving. Planned and habitual giving reminds us of our dependence on God, enabling us to let go of our security blankets which provide us with the illusion of independence. Habitual giving also sensitizes us to the needs of others, while acquiring possessions focuses attention on ourselves. Generosity is a bridge to the future; acquiring possessions is a fortress to shield us against the future and to protect the fragile present. Generosity seeks to engage the world and to work with it; acquiring possessions seeks to conform the world to us and our desires. Finally, generosity is responsive to the inner voice of the spirit; acquiring possessions muffles and ignores it.

Detachment is the ability to hold on to things with a loose grip. That's what is at the heart of the spirit of poverty that is practiced by vowed religious in the Catholic tradition. It does not mean that religious people are called to wear rags. Rather, it means a personal detachment from the goods owned by the community as a whole. Jesus said that it is easier for a camel to pass through the eye of a needle than for a rich person to enter the kingdom of heaven. He doesn't say, however, that it is impossible. All of us, especially those who may be quite well off, need to recognize the inherent dangers of wealth and possessions. It is only through detachment that we are able to grow closer to the kingdom of God. While society is constantly urging us to acquire more and more, detachment is the ability to say, "I have enough."

How to be content with what you have

Here are three suggestions for developing a spirit of detachment, which, in essence, is the ability to be content with what you have.

Get serious about observing the Lord's Day (even if you don't go to church).

Instead of thinking of Sunday as the day that helps you get ready for the important work of *producing* during the week, think of the work week as the experience that helps you get ready for the chance to enjoy *being* on Sunday. Sunday is a day to step off of the merry-go-round of producing and consuming in order to recognize how blessed we truly are. This leads to a spirit of contentment, which enables us to practice detachment. Sunday should be a day that focuses less on acquiring and more on experiencing. It is a day for taking long walks, visiting family and friends, going to shows or concerts, enjoying a good book, or just sitting back and enjoying the fact that you're busy doing nothing. It is not a day to get ahead, but a day to allow yourself to be right where you are, which is where God is found.

Learn to be patient and overcome impulsiveness.

Much of our consumerism is driven by impulsiveness. We see; therefore, we buy. We find it hard to wait when we can possess something right now. It's interesting to note how often Scripture encourages us to wait. In Psalm 27:14 the psalmist says, "Wait for the LORD; be strong, and let your heart take courage; wait for the LORD!" Our desire to possess is fueled by impulsiveness. By waiting you can overcome the impulse to buy; it will go away, much as hunger pangs pass if you turn your attention to something else. As a result, you'll be better able to differentiate between buying what you need and what you want.

Practice simplicity.

More does not necessarily equal *better*. The fact is that the more you acquire and the more you possess, the more complicated your life will be. One of the ways that you can foster a spirit of detachment in your life is to practice simplicity. Again, this doesn't mean that you have to wear a tunic and sandals. It simply means that by cutting down on the clutter in your life, you will be able to focus more clearly on trusting God rather than your possessions. This folksy tale further illustrates this point.

A hard-working businessman spotted a fisherman sitting lazily beside his boat. He scoffed at his laziness asking, "Why aren't you out there fishing?" The fisherman replied, "Because I've caught enough fish for today." The businessman laughed and said, "You have no business sense. You could get way ahead of your competitors by catching more fish than you need." The fisherman looked puzzled and asked, "What would I do with the extra fish?" The businessman rolled his eyes and replied, "You could double your profits and invest in a bigger and better boat and some nylon nets so that you could catch even more fish. Before long, you'd have a whole fleet and would be rich like me." The fisherman still looked puzzled. "What would I do then?" he asked. The wealthy businessman smugly replied, "You'd be able to sit back and enjoy life." "That's what I'm doing right now!" replied the fisherman.

Simplicity means being able to say, "I have enough. I don't need anything else right now." In fact, not only do most of us have enough, but we probably have too much. When we realize that, we can practice detachment and give away some of our possessions, bringing a little more simplicity into our lives.

How to use what you have

When we hold on loosely to what we have, we are ready for the next challenge—*using* what we have. A key to a healthy spirituality is maintaining balance when it comes to material goods and wealth. Everyone has to find their own point of balance; there are no rules for it. Here are seven principles that can help you find your balance point.

Deepen your appreciation of God's creation.

God created the world and he invites *all* of his children to have dominion over and enjoy his material creation. But we're not to abuse it. Today more than ever we are becoming increasingly aware of the fragility of creation and of our responsibility for reducing our carbon footprints. A deeper appreciation for God's creation leads us to care for all God has made. Our spiritual wellness is intimately connected with the well-being of God's creation.

Deepen your awareness of the sanctity of all human life.

We hold in great esteem what we label as precious. Spiritual wellness demands that we view all human life—from the womb to the tomb—as precious. A lack of respect for the dignity of the human being threatens not only our spiritual well-being but also the foundation of a moral vision for society. A deepened respect for all human life leads us to respect and value people over material goods.

Resist excessive individualism.

American society worships individualism. On the other hand, spiritual wellness thrives on social interaction. Human beings grow and flourish best when participating in community life, subordinating our needs to the needs of the many. A healthy spirituality fosters a deep concern for the common good.

Balance your right to purchase and possess with the responsibility to give and share.

In the Gospel of Luke, Jesus says, "From everyone to whom much has been given, much will be required; and from the one to whom much has been entrusted, even more will be demanded" (Luke 12:48). Jesus does not condemn those who have, but he strongly warns them of the perilous waters they are navigating and suggests that they use what they have to help those who are have-nots. Spiritual wellness is threatened when *having* is not balanced by *giving*.

See reality from the perspective of those who have less.

Pope Leo XIII taught that once the demands of necessity and propriety have been fulfilled, the rest of one's wealth belongs to the poor. Yikes! That's thought provoking. This teaching shows why it is a good practice to ask whether we *need* what we are about to buy or just want it. The fact is that too many people continue to live in dire poverty even though this is the richest period in human history. Spiritual wellness relies on our ability to make the needs of those who are poor and vulnerable a priority in our lives. This is why Scripture called for a practice known as the Jubilee Year (Leviticus 25). Every fifty years debts were to be canceled, prisoners were to be freed, and land was to be returned to its original owners. In this way the playing field could be leveled and hope could be restored for those who were downtrodden. This dream never quite became a reality in ancient Judaism as far as we can tell. However, Jesus begins his ministry by reviving the concept when he says:

> The Spirit of the Lord is upon me,
>   because he has anointed me to bring good news to
>   the poor.
> He has sent me to proclaim release to the captives
>   and recovery of sight to the blind,
>   to let the oppressed go free,
> to proclaim the year of the Lord's favor.

—Luke 4:18–19

Jesus is not suggesting that this Jubilee Year be observed every fifty years. He was announcing it as a new reality in which we are called to live—the kingdom of God. He was ushering in a perpetual Jubilee in which the poor are no longer ignored. It is this concept that led Fr. Pedro Arrupe, SJ, then the Father General of the Jesuits, to coin the phrase "a preferential option for the poor" to describe the way Catholics are called to relate to the poor. This is the standard established by Jesus when he indicated that we will be judged according to how we treat those who are poor and vulnerable (Matthew 25:31–46).

Recognize the dignity of work.

Spiritual wellness relies on the recognition that having a job is not merely a way to make money but is an important way to participate in God's creation and to use one's gifts in the service of others. Work has dignity, and all people have the right to productive work, fair wages, and private property, the right to organize, join unions, and pursue economic opportunity. Spiritual wellness leads us to recognize that the economy is meant to serve people, and not the other way around.

Practice solidarity with others.

Spiritual wellness depends on our ability to recognize the needs of others and to stand with them during their time of trial. That's known as practicing solidarity—the awareness that, because God is our Father, we are all brothers and sisters with the responsibility to care for one another. Through the incarnation of Jesus, God stands in solidarity with humanity, dwelling among us. As followers of Christ, we are called to stand in solidarity with others. Solidarity unites rich and poor, weak and strong, and helps create a society that recognizes our interdependence. In today's global village, we recognize that solidarity has global dimensions.

Why we need the poor

Some years ago Francis Cardinal George, as Archbishop of Chicago, said to a group of major donors, "The poor need you to draw them out of poverty." He then said something that took everyone by surprise: "And *you* need the poor to keep you out of hell!" Some people thought he was being facetious, but anyone familiar with Cardinal George knew that he meant precisely what he said. Those wealthy people who were donating large sums of money to the Church were sharing their abundance as God intended. To do otherwise would be to ignore the will of God. Hell is simply that state of being that rejects God's will, which amounts to a rejection of God's loving presence, now and eternally.

Sharing does not come easily for most of us. We are born completely self-centered. As infants we cry in order to have all of our needs met. As we learn to speak, one of the first words we grasp after "Mama" and "Dada" is "Mine!" As we grow our parents make their best effort to increase our vocabulary by one more very important word: "Share!" As adults we have to learn that there's plenty to go around. God's creation is filled with everything we need, all provided by a generous and loving God who calls us to share likewise with others. Jesus' first miracle, the changing of water into wine at the wedding feast at Cana, reinforces this notion of abundance. Six huge water jars, each capable of holding twenty to thirty gallons, are filled to the brim with the finest wine. The message? For those who live under God's reign there is plenty of goodness to share.

Stewards of God's creation

Recognizing the abundance of God's creation is the first step toward developing a generous spirit. The second step is realizing that when it comes to material possessions, the word "mine" is a misnomer. There is really no such thing as "mine," because everything in God's creation truly belongs to God. He has chosen, in his generous love, to share it with us. We are not "owners" but "stewards."

In the Nicene Creed we proclaim our belief in God as the Creator of "all things visible and invisible." In this Creed we express our belief that everything we have is a gift from God. Our response is to live as stewards of God's gifts and to use them wisely for the good of all. Since we are entrusted with the care of that which belongs to God, we avoid hoarding anything for ourselves. Stewardship calls us to care responsibly for God's gifts and to share generously of our time, talents, and treasure.

We practice stewardship by sharing our *time* with others, realizing that we are all living on "borrowed time." We share our *talents* in service of others, knowing that our talents are gifts from God. We share our *treasure,* our material possessions, acknowledging that the resources of the earth were created by God for the good of all people.

Stewardship, then, is not about money. It is an approach to spirituality. It is an attitude that enhances our relationships with God and with our brothers and sisters by calling us to center our lives on God rather than on ourselves.

Our declaration of dependence

When you stop to think about it, the one prayer that Jesus composed and taught his followers to pray, the Our Father, is the antidote to excessive materialism. Jesus knows that we acquire possessions—these security blankets—in order to compensate for the insecurities and fears that come with our imagined independence. Let's face it; possessing the means to provide for ourselves is easier than trusting in God. So to help us trust, Jesus offers us a prayer that can become our "Declaration of *De*pendence."

At the heart of the Lord's Prayer are seven petitions. They dispel any illusion of self-sufficiency, in favor of total dependence on and trust in a loving parent whom we call *Abba*, a term of intimacy similar to "Papa" or "Momma" used by children. What need have we of security blankets when we can turn to a Divine Parent whose love will most assuredly provide for us? In particular, at the heart of the petitions we pray in the Our Father is the petition for "our daily bread." This is the confident request for God to provide us with what we need.

In the end, it's all about letting go instead of holding on. That's why Jesus said that the greatest love—the most generous act of all—is to lay down one's life for another. To lay down one's life simply means to let go of yourself, to trust, and to generously put the good of others before your own. That can only be done when we hold on loosely to the things of this world. Whenever we do so, our soul gets a taste of what it means to return to Eden, that place of total trust and dependence.

Recognizing and Setting Limits

What scratches your itch?

One summer evening I sat outdoors with three of my brothers, my sister, and her family. It was a nice night and I went with the "shoeless Joe" look. The mosquitoes feasted on my ankles, insteps, and shins. Over the next week, I itched terribly. I furiously scratched away at the bites, attempting to find some relief. Scratching felt so good! But relief didn't last. I scratched so often and so hard that I broke the skin on each little bite. I spent much of the rest of the summer walking around with tiny little scabs and then scars dotting my legs. We can scratch all we want, but sometimes what we really need is an antihistamine!

On a spiritual level, we all have an itch. It's that chronic, gnawing sense of discomfort that begs for a scratch. Most of the time we don't identify the source of the itch. We just scratch. And scratch. And scratch. We find ways to bring about temporary relief. But it's only temporary. We often scratch to excess, breaking the "skin" of our soul and causing harm to ourselves without eliminating the source of said itch.

Itches—and how we scratch them

Spiritual itches occur when life, like a giant mosquito, takes a bite out of us.

- We face the breakup of a relationship
- We lose a loved one
- We lose a job
- We're overlooked for a promotion
- We suffer a financial loss
- We endure a difficult life transition
- We fail at an important task
- We witness meaningless pain and suffering
- We experience general chaos
- We endure seemingly hopeless situations

Some of these experiences are immediate, tragic, and painful. Others are subtle, ongoing, and mildly frustrating. All of them cause an itch that must be scratched. We want to feel good, so we

- shop
- eat
- drink alcohol
- use drugs
- gamble

- smoke
- exercise
- have sex
- play video games
- blog, tweet, surf the Internet
- watch television
- work

Most of these are normal, everyday activities which, done in moderation, are enjoyable and healthy ways of taking joy in life's pleasures. We do them because we want to feel good. Is that too much to ask? Well, yes and no.

Pleasures can get out of hand

On the one hand, God created us to take pleasure in his creation. Through our senses—taste, touch, smell, sight, sound—we are able to take in a myriad of pleasures. A healthy spirituality relishes these pleasures. In fact, Catholic spirituality *celebrates* these pleasures. Our liturgical calendar is resplendent with feasts. Our greatest feast, Easter, is celebrated with a fifty-day festival!

On the other hand, danger comes when one of these pleasurable activities drifts toward excess. We can become *addicted*. This term is usually applied to abuse of alcohol or drugs, but now it describes dependence on many substances and behaviors. Today, we realize that addictions (dependencies) can occur in a variety of behaviors, all of which share one thing in common: they are designed to bring about pleasure.

There are two ways to identify when a behavior has crossed over into excess.

The behavior has become counterproductive. You don't enjoy shopping anymore because you are spending money you don't have. You're depressed while watching television or surfing the Web because you know you're doing too much of it. You don't enjoy a good meal anymore because you're overweight from eating too many good meals. So much for cheering yourself up.

The behavior has become persistent. Even though the behavior doesn't help anymore, you do it anyway. You shop, drink, eat, gamble even more, hoping the old magic will return.

Excesses like these do not necessarily cause our lives to crumble all around us. In fact, we can continue on engaging in these practices and continually getting a charge out of them. The danger is becoming *dependent* on these behaviors to scratch the itch in our soul. We have convinced ourselves that we need to do this particular thing in order to feel good. Spiritually, we have handed over control of our inner happiness to a substance or behavior. We come to believe that our overall enjoyment of life depends on this one behavior instead of on God and his creation.

In addition to limiting our overall enjoyment of life, these addictions often do damage over time. They can lead to:

- physical effects that accompany excessive eating, drinking, exercising
- depression, mood swings
- financial burdens
- neglect of other responsibilities
- strain on relationships
- apathy

- guilt
- low self-esteem

The effect of excesses can be subtle. Thomas Keating, a Trappist monk, points out that those of us who are not involved in "obvious addictions" often fail to realize that many of our behaviors are compulsive, and that we are "blissfully unaware of how powerless we are because we can usually fulfill the basic obligations of life."

Getting comfortably numb

Spiritual wellness is tied up with our cravings. Our cravings for food, drink, and other substances and behaviors are symptoms of a deeper craving. We ingest caffeine, nicotine, alcohol, or other chemicals, and gamble, shop, and work too hard in order to get a temporary fix—a few moments of feeling alive. These ways of satisfying our cravings prevent us from truly feeling our feelings. They subtly and gradually dull our senses making us "comfortably numb," as the famous Pink Floyd song put it.

St. Augustine, the great Church Father, illustrates this human habit vividly. As a young man he sought a myriad of ways to scratch the gnawing itch in his soul. After experimenting with many vices and a few philosophies, he realized that the hunger he felt could only be satisfied by God. Thus his famous saying, "Our hearts are restless, Lord, until they find rest in you." Even after this realization, Augustine continued to struggle. This led to another famous quote, "Lord, make me chaste—but not yet." In contemporary times, rock star Bruce Springsteen captured this problem when he sang, "Everybody's got a hungry heart." How we attempt to satisfy that hunger—how we scratch the itch—is a key to spiritual wellness.

The wisdom of the Twelve Steps

Most people struggle with dependency on things that fail to satisfy their spiritual hunger. For some people this dependency becomes a serious addiction that needs drastic measures. In his book *Divine Therapy and Addiction*, the Trappist Thomas Keating says that people who enter recovery programs are, in a sense, more fortunate than people who remain comfortably numb in their dependencies. When people enter recovery, they can find help in a Twelve-Step program.

All of us can learn something from the Twelve Steps. They were first written in the 1930s as the basis for the recovery program called Alcoholics Anonymous. Since then, the Twelve Steps have served as the basis for recovery programs aimed at people addicted to drugs, food, sex, gambling, and other disorders.

Here are the Twelve Steps as written by the founders of Alcoholics Anonymous:

1. We admitted we were powerless over alcohol—that our lives had become unmanageable.

2. Came to believe that a Power greater than ourselves could restore us to sanity.

3. Made a decision to turn our will and our lives over to the care of God as we understood Him.

4. Made a searching and fearless moral inventory of ourselves.

5. Admitted to God, to ourselves, and to another human being the exact nature of our wrongs.

6. Were entirely ready to have God remove all these defects of character.

7. Humbly asked Him to remove our shortcomings.

8. Made a list of all persons we had harmed, and became willing to make amends to them all.

9. Made direct amends to such people wherever possible, except when to do so would injure them or others.

10. Continued to take personal inventory and when we were wrong, promptly admitted it.

11. Sought through prayer and meditation to improve our conscious contact with God as we understood Him, praying only for knowledge of His will for us and the power to carry that out.

12. Having had a spiritual awakening as the result of these steps, we tried to carry this message to alcoholics, and to practice these principles in all our affairs.

Two insights in the Twelve Steps stand out.

Honesty is essential

The Twelve Steps cut to the chase, requiring those who seek recovery to name the "sin" that has taken control of their lives. There's no room for denial. The individual must admit the problem to him or herself, to God, and to at least one other human being. Unless we name the reality and admit that we are not in control, we remain trapped by it, and recovery is not possible.

We're powerless

The Twelve Steps teach us to admit powerlessness over our problem. We are not in control. We cannot make the itch go away by simply willing ourselves to stop scratching. Until we admit powerlessness over whatever negative behavior we are trapped in and come face to face with it, any of our efforts at recovery will be as successful as laying cement during a rainstorm. Good luck with that. Our problem holds the key to our wellness. When we know we are powerless, we can let God in.

Stay alive and thirsty

Spiritual wellness is about facing and integrating our imperfections, not removing them. Our negative behaviors dull our awareness. Spiritual wellness is about being awake. It is about paying attention to your thirst, not drowning yourself in an effort to quench it. To borrow a line from a famous beer commercial, the key to a healthy spirituality is to "stay thirsty, my friends."

In his book *The Journey of Desire,* John Eldridge says that we face three choices when it comes to scratching our itch:

- We can be dead (in total denial of our itch).
- We can be addicted (engaging in behaviors that make us comfortably numb).
- We can be alive and thirsty.

Eldridge writes, "To live in thirst is to live with an ache. Every addiction comes from the attempt to get rid of the ache." He paraphrases the great philosopher Pascal:

> You can be satisfied, you just can't be sated. There is a great joy in a glass of cabernet; the whole bottle is another thing. The Israelites tried to hoard the manna—and it crawled with maggots. Our soul's insatiable desire becomes the venom . . . when it demands its fill here and now, through the otherwise beautiful and good gifts of our lives.

Scratch the itch the right way

So just what are we to do with these itches, these micro-addictions, disordered behaviors, and unhealthy habits? Let's look at some strategies.

Recognize and honor your limits

Not everyone who has a drink after a hard day is an alcoholic. Not everyone who has a piece of chocolate when they're feeling down has an eating disorder. Not everyone who goes shopping after a long week at work is a shopaholic. We avoid abusing these things by recognizing limits.

My Dad almost always had a beer when he came home from a long day at work, but I never saw him drink two beers. My wife likes to keep a box of chocolates in the house and craves them, especially after a stressful day. She always takes out one piece of chocolate, eats it, and puts the box away. My mother-in-law enjoyed going to the casino—but always with a modest amount of money. When it was gone, she left.

If we have a particular weakness for any of these pleasures, we should recognize it, embrace it, and announce it to others: "I'll have a beer with you but don't let me order a refill!" "I love the casino but make sure I stop at $__." "Ooh, that dessert looks good . . . just cut me a sliver though." If you recognize your limits and embrace them, you can proudly announce them to others so that everyone can see what they already knew—you, like all other people, are broken.

Pray regularly

Practice an extended period of private prayer, reflection, meditation, pondering, percolating—whatever you want to call it. But do *something* on a regular basis to engage in a conscious dialogue with your inner self and with God. If every waking moment is crowded with input and stimulation, your soul's voice is being drowned out. You'll eventually begin to experience spiritual numbness . . . a blasé feeling. Without prayer, you run the risk of avoiding issues that may lead you to self-destructive thoughts, feelings, and behaviors. Not making time to pay attention to your soul each day is like driving around with God in the back seat of the car, but with the music turned on so loud that you can't hear a word he's saying.

One of the simplest ways of getting in touch with your soul on a daily basis is to practice the Daily Examen, a method of prayer that was taught by St. Ignatius of Loyola. (See the outline of the Examen on page 12.) By praying this way, you become more aware of how God has been present to you in the past and therefore, more attuned to how he is acting in the present. It's like turning down the volume on the car stereo and asking God, "I'm sorry, did you say something?" This practice does not typically result in some kind of ecstasy or ongoing feeling of euphoria. It simply puts us in touch with what our soul is pondering (often without our conscious awareness); thus, it enables us to avoid behaviors that bring only temporary relief from the gnawing itch at our core. The result is that our soul grows and we generally feel more alive.

Be honest and contrite

Our disordered actions are bad enough. The only thing worse is the denial, rationalization, lying, and callousness that we often engage in to cover them up. Eventually, we come to believe the lie and we convince ourselves that we don't need help—an attitude that is one of the main obstacles to spiritual wellness.

Jesus called people with this attitude "righteous" (Luke 18:9). He said that sinners and outcasts were closer to the kingdom of God because they usually were all-too-aware of their weaknesses and need for salvation. The wall of self-righteousness prevents us from encountering God's mercy, which he is always ready to offer to us. Contrition and honesty remove the bricks of the wall of righteousness so that it eventually collapses, allowing God's mercy to flow in. Like President Reagan saying, "Mr. Gorbachev, tear down this wall!" in reference to the oppressive Berlin Wall, God is daily inviting us to tear down the walls we build in our souls when we engage in behaviors that impede honesty and contrition. In the spirituality of Alcoholics Anonymous, sobriety is only ten percent about alcohol and ninety percent about honesty. The solution is not to beat ourselves up over our failures; it is to simply, contritely, and honestly admit that we are broken and need fixing.

The Sacrament of Penance and Reconciliation helps us stay honest and contrite. Sadly, many people avoid the sacrament, thinking they do not need to confess their sins to a priest. Ironically, many of them find themselves publicly confessing in front of a room full of people at Twelve-Step meetings, where contrition and brutal honesty are nonnegotiables. Grace finds a way.

Practice charity and self-sacrifice

One of the most effective ways of overcoming self-indulgent behaviors is to focus less attention on yourself and more on the needs of others. Service to others forces us into a selfless mode. When we engage in charitable works, our spiritual itch lessens. Why? Not simply because we are keeping busy, but because our spirit transcends the narrow borders of our own life. Engaging in self-sacrificing behaviors does not necessarily make us feel happy. In fact, they often can make us feel sad about the plight of others. However, the soul appreciates authentic feelings instead of the superficialities we often feed it. Spiritual health is not about being happy all the time; it is about experiencing authentic feelings and being alive.

Get involved with the poor

Working with the poor and marginalized helps us recognize the part of ourselves that is poor and marginalized. We realize that very little separates us from those we are serving. Serving the poor helps us more than our helping them. Such encounters awaken our soul and bring us face-to-face with our own brokenness. We can run away, not wanting to face anything that might make us sad, or we can humbly recognize our own brokenness reflected in those we serve. We can pray for the grace we need to allow ourselves to be fixed, not through our own efforts but through the power of God.

Get involved with a faith community

The problem with being "spiritual but not religious" is that it usually means living without a community. It certainly can be a spiritual experience to walk through the woods instead of going to church. But the woods don't challenge us to change our lives, which is what a faith community can do.

My friend Andrew and his wife were unhappy with their home parish in a comfortable middle-class suburb of Chicago. They joined a parish in one of the poorest areas of Joliet, Illinois, far from their home. Andrew says, "The pastor there leaves us disturbed by the gospel. He reminds us that our response to those who are poor should not be on our terms and at our pace. He is like a John the Baptist who yells at us and loves us enough to tell us the truth. He brings to us the urgency of the gospel. It all disturbs us and makes us more Catholic." Andrew and his wife could have simply stopped going to church. Instead, they chose to be disturbed.

We need a faith community to challenge us to grow into the people we are called to be. Too many faith communities settle for being places where everybody feels good. A true faith community proclaims the gospel of Jesus, which begins, at least in the Gospel of Mark, with the word, "Repent!" The gospel message is all about conversion—a change of heart and mind. Faith communities that are alive challenge us to do the hard work needed to discover the only salve that will heal us—the grace of our Lord Jesus Christ.

Participate in ritual worship

Healthy spirituality explores mystery and encounters a transformative power that is beyond human capacity. The rituals, signs, symbols, and gestures of Catholic worship speak a language of mystery. They touch realities beyond the intellectual and rational. We can't think our itches away. Words alone cannot penetrate the place deep in our being where the itch resides. Only a language of mystery can soothe the discomfort we carry within.

Ritual works. Human beings respond deeply to ritual actions. That's why only the ritual action of a kiss could awaken Sleeping Beauty. Kisses work. Kissing your spouse daily helps sustain a marriage. The ritual action of the Eucharist sustains our spiritual life. Do marriages sometimes get boring? Yes. Does the Mass sometimes get boring? Yes. But the rituals continue to nourish us.

Change your routine

Often we can avoid trouble by physically removing ourselves from troublesome places and conditions. Too often we let our "inner kids" run wild in the candy stores of life. If you're spending too much time on the Internet, watching television, engaging in social media, or playing video games, then you literally need to get out of the house. If you can't avoid the box of donuts in the lunch room at work during your break, head out the door for a ten-minute walk. You won't be able to engage in unhealthy behaviors if those behaviors reside in another "zip code."

My friend Kate begins every day, no matter what the weather (and we live in Chicago, mind you) by standing outside in her backyard for at least fifteen minutes. (Luckily, her husband built her a little shelter to protect her from rain and snow.) This reminds her that to remain spiritually healthy, she needs to turn down the volume on life and pay attention to her soul. Does she still use the Internet, social media, watch television, and so on? Yes. However, her daily routine of standing outside keeps her from allowing any of those distractions from masquerading as the real thing.

Forgive yourself and resist perfection

Our cravings are very powerful. That's not surprising, because ultimately those cravings are for God. They get misdirected to food, alcohol, shopping, gambling, sexual gratification, and many other things. But they are strong, and they are hard to overcome. Try as we may, we will fail from time to time. When this happens, don't beat yourself up. Feelings of guilt and shame will only worsen the craving. Instead, be honest and contrite with yourself, with God, and with some other person, and get on with your life. Forgive yourself. Be gentle and give yourself another chance because God would never think of doing less for you.

Practice disorder displacement

You probably learned about water displacement in science class in school. You can measure the volume of an object by putting it in a tank of water. It "displaces" water—that is, it forces water up. When you measure how much water it displaces, you'll know its volume.

You can displace negative behaviors by displacing them with positive behaviors. One of the most effective ways to do this is by focusing on gratitude. Often, when I feel compelled to engage in some behavior that is vapid at best and negative at worst, I make a gratitude list. I make a list of all the things I am grateful for. Once you start, it's hard to stop. You quickly begin to realize just how blessed you are and how grateful you are for these blessings. Before you know it, the gratitude has literally displaced any feelings of discontent. It's very scientific!

Desires are not bad, but they can cause us to lose balance in life if left unchecked. Practicing moderation—setting limits—is the key to spiritual wellness. It's not easy to be moderate today in anything, from politics to food! Living in moderation is a countercultural statement in a consumerist society that screams "Supersize me!" Setting limits does not reduce your capacity for joy nor does it enslave you. Rather, it sets you free to enjoy life more fully and more deeply. Instead of watching your waistline, your debt, or your hangovers grow, you'll be "watching" your soul grow nobler.

A minor exorcism for people who miss the mark

Since we have been talking about mini-addictions, I'd like to conclude with a minor exorcism of the Catholic Church—a prayer for minor disorders. Thanks to Hollywood, we know all about major, full-blown exorcisms of the Linda Blair, Anthony Hopkins variety. Minor exorcisms are much more common. There's even an exorcism prayer in the Rite of Baptism for Children.

The exorcism prayer here is adapted from the Rite of Christian Initiation of Adults. It recognizes that each of us falls prey to mini-addictions—those negative behaviors that prevent us from truly knowing ourselves, others, and God. We miss the mark when it comes to connecting with God. In fact, *missing the mark* is the literal translation of the Greek word for *sin*, which is used in the New Testament.

> God of power,
> you created us in your image and likeness
> and formed us in holiness and justice.
> Even when we sinned against you,
> you did not abandon us,
> but in your wisdom chose to save us by the incarnation
>   of your Son.
> Save me, your servant:
> free me from evil and the tyranny of the enemy.
> Keep far from me the spirit of wickedness,
> falsehood, and greed.
> Receive me into your kingdom
> and open my heart to understand your Gospel,
> so that, as a child of the light,
> I may live as a member of your Church,
> bear witness to your truth,
> and put into practice your commands of love.

KEY 6

Seeking Beauty

Where is your dream vacation spot?

Is it the stunning alpine valleys of New Zealand? The natural beauty and ancient history of Greece? The magical Inca temples of Peru? The stunning beauty and Polynesian flavor of the Hawaiian Islands? The sparkling white sandy beaches of the Caribbean? The architectural majesty and romance of Paris?

Whatever your choice, chances are it has something to do with *beauty*. We are drawn to beauty. When vacation time rolls around, we seek to refresh our bodies, minds, and souls by encountering beauty. We do this because we need beauty. We need beauty just as much as we need proper nutrition in our diet. Think about the times that you "have a taste" for some food—for steak, a fresh tomato, an orange. This is the body's way of calling out for required nutrients. In the same way, the human soul craves beauty. Spiritual wellness requires a steady diet of beauty. We are drawn to beauty, attracted by its splendor, and enticed by its appeal.

Where can we find transcendence?

Human beings believe that beauty can transport us some-where. I'm not talking about "Beam me up, Scotty" trans-portation from one planet to another as depicted in *Star Trek*. The kind of transporting that I'm talking about is synonym-ous with transcendence. We desire to transcend ourselves—to be transported beyond the merely physical and material to an experience of the spiritual. We seek to touch mystery and to be touched by it. That which is beautiful possesses mystery. So we are attracted to beauty in hopes that we will be able to touch mystery and, in doing so, be loved and embraced by it.

Much of the beauty of God's creation—sunrises and sun-sets, ocean waves, exotic plants and animals, and majestic mountains—is only experienced from a distance. We, as human beings, have access to beauty in a closer way: through another human being. We are drawn to the human beings we find attractive because we want to encounter mystery, and mystery is beautiful.

Think about how human beings are attracted to one another. Typically, attraction begins on the external level. We take notice of a person's age, their gender, their ethnicity, and their various physical traits such as height, weight, com-plexion, hair and eye color, shape, and build. The quest for beauty does not stop there, however. We next begin to search for internal beauty. We explore hobbies, major beliefs, recre-ational preferences, and other traits while also paying atten-tion to demeanors, attitudes, and level of intelligence. We do all of this to encounter beauty, to both possess and be pos-sessed by it.

God invented sex

The wonderful thing about the beauty of other human beings is that we can unite with that beauty in the most intimate way. It's called sex. In particular, it is that most intimate of expressions—sexual intercourse—that holds the promise of transporting us beyond ourselves and into that encounter with mystery that we long for so deeply.

While sex is one of the greatest gifts we enjoy as human beings, it is also something that can cause us much grief. The beauty of nature is accessible to anyone who wants to indulge in it; the beauty of other human beings is not ours for the taking. There are complex rules and protocols surrounding human sexuality that protect the beauty we desire. Sex itself is not the problem. It's our approach to sex that gets us into trouble. God invented sex. God is not embarrassed by sex. Dare we say that God delights in sex? Why else would he give this gift to us and direct his Church to celebrate it as a sacrament? Precisely because the act of sex between a husband and wife is a reflection of the passionate love that God has for his people.

An entire book of the Bible, Song of Solomon, is about the passionate sexual desire between spouses. The words *God*, *Lord*, and *Yahweh* are not found in this steamy book of the Bible. These words are found in abundance: kisses, breasts, bed, lips, neck, tongue, legs, neck, navel, flowing locks, fire, and wine. If the Song of Solomon were made into a movie, it would definitely be rated R. The inclusion of this book in the Bible can be attributed to nothing other than the fact that the intimacy of sexual relations is a gift that comes to us from God. Any discussion of sex must use this as its starting point.

Sex goes awry

It didn't take long for us to take this gift of God and distort it in our never-ending quest to find a shortcut to beauty and transcendence. A man who epitomizes this tendency is none other than one of Jesus' forefathers: the great King David. David had an eye for beauty; unfortunately, his royal eye landed upon the beauty of another man's wife.

David gets up from his couch one day and takes a stroll on the roof of his palace. His gaze is captured by a beautiful woman bathing. David inquires and discovers that she is Bathsheba, the wife of Uriah the Hittite who is away in battle. David sends for the woman and has sex with her. Worse, when he later discovers that Bathsheba is pregnant with his child, David orders that Uriah be placed in the front lines of battle, where he is struck down and killed. Talk about scandal! Of course, not all such scandals are relegated to the Old Testament. Just look at this list of names:

- Tiger Woods
- Bill Clinton
- John F. Kennedy
- Ali McGraw
- LeAnn Rimes
- Gary Hart
- Jimmy Swaggart
- Jennifer Garner
- Newt Gingrich
- Ingrid Bergman
- Eliot Spitzer
- Jennifer Lopez

- Mark Sanford
- John Edwards
- Princess Diana
- Arnold Schwarzenegger
- Meg Ryan
- David Letterman
- Eddie Murphy
- Hugh Grant

All of these people have been involved in very public sex scandals—emphasis on the word *public*. There are countless illicit sexual liaisons happening under the radar. In our quest for authentic beauty, we are all too eager to settle for sexual shortcuts that lead us astray. These sexual shortcuts ignore the reality that human beings are essentially psychosomatic beings: what happens to the body (*soma*) is intimately connected to the soul (*psyche*) and vice versa. Ironically, we are becoming a society that separates body and soul when it comes to sexuality, while also demanding holistic health care that takes emotional, mental, and spiritual factors into account when treating illness.

"Friends with benefits" doesn't work

It is within this context that the phenomenon of "friends with benefits" has grown in popularity. The *Urban Dictionary* describes this as "two friends who have a sexual relationship without being emotionally involved." The friends simply engage in casual sex "without a monogamous relationship or any kind of commitment." The idea of "friends with benefits" was the topic of an episode of *Seinfeld*, one of my all-time favorite television shows. Jerry and Elaine concoct a set of rules designed to allow them to continue their friendship (which they refer to as "this"), while enjoying sex without any commitment or emotional attachment (which they refer to as "that"). Their goal is to keep *this* and *that* separate. They make rules designed to enable them to continue their friendship while enjoying sex with no strings attached:

- no kiss good-bye after sex
- sleeping over after sex is optional
- no phone call the day after sex

They discover that keeping *this* and *that* separate is impossible. Jerry and Elaine quickly discover that sex inevitably brings emotional entanglements they sought to avoid. It's a rule of life: it's impossible to tip-toe in and out of the sexual garden of someone else's life without disturbing the roots of the delicate plants that thrive there.

This is precisely why societies have always had taboos on sex outside of marriage—in order to preserve the act of sexual intercourse as the highest expression of intimacy. This frees us to explore a myriad of other appropriate ways to express intimacy, create true emotional bonds, and thus, experience beauty. "Friends with benefits" breaks that taboo in an effort to side-step real intimacy and just grasp at the illusion of beauty.

"Cold shower" spirituality doesn't work either

Desire is not the problem. The problem is where we aim that desire. The solution is not to squelch our desires. I am not a big fan of what I call "cold-shower" spirituality—an approach that tells us to "just say no" without giving us anything to say "yes" to. When we experience strong sexual desires, we're supposed to grit our teeth, grab a Bible, and read passages about self-control while chanting to ourselves, "I will NOT be horny. I will NOT be horny. I will NOT be horny." Repressing desires leads to an unhealthy spirituality. If sin is indeed "missing the mark," then we need strategies for *hitting* the mark. Sitting on the sidelines of life and congratulating ourselves for avoiding temptation is not a healthy spirituality.

Sexual desires are like a strong riptide that wants to sweep us out to sea. When encountering a strong riptide, we can just surrender and let the current take us out to sea. At first, there will be a rush of excitement as we experience the power of the waves, but eventually we will find ourselves in over our heads. Another option is to desperately swim against the current. We may make some headway, but eventually we will exhaust ourselves and the current will carry us away. Another option is to stay out of the ocean altogether, and sometimes we must do that. However, the ocean is there to be enjoyed; we shouldn't just watch from the shore. The best way to handle a strong riptide is to swim parallel to the shore, away from the undertow, thus allowing the waves to carry you back in.

Similarly, a healthy spirituality means neither repressing desires nor impulsively surrendering to them. We need to do more than say no to something. We need to say a resounding YES to something greater. And that something greater is indeed, beauty. Not glamour, as the world offers, but *true beauty*.

This kind of beauty is found in intimacy, a true delving into the depths of mystery that is another person's heart and soul. Intimacy is not to be equated with sexual activity. We can be intimate with any number of people and not have sex with them. Spiritual wellness depends on *seeking the kind of beauty that can only be found in an intimate relationship*. And there are no shortcuts.

Our desire for beauty
is a desire for God

Here's the point: beauty can be equated with God just as truth and goodness are equated with God. Ultimately, our desire for beauty is a desire to be intimate with God, who is the source of all beauty. Think about it. If God is the Creator of the universe, and if God existed before he called the universe into being, then beauty resided in God from time immemorial.

Scripture is full of references to God's beauty. King David prayed these words:

> One thing I asked of the LORD,
>   that will I seek after;
> to live in the house of the LORD
>   all the days of my life,
> to behold the beauty of the LORD,
>   and to inquire in his temple.
>
> —Psalm 27:4

Throughout Scripture we read of the desire to "see" God "face-to-face". This is poetic language for an encounter with God that brings satisfaction and delight in the same way that beauty does.

> If my people who are called by my name humble themselves, pray, **seek my face**, and turn from their wicked ways, then I will hear from heaven, and will forgive their sin and heal their land.
>
> —2 Chronicles 7:14

"Come," my heart says, "seek his **face**!"
　　Your **face**, LORD, do I seek.
　　Do not hide your **face** from me.

　　　　　　　　　　　　—Psalm 27:8–9

I will return again to my place
　　until they acknowledge their guilt and seek my **face.**

　　　　　　　　　　　　—Hosea 5:15

God's "face" refers to his presence, and to be in God's presence is an intensely beautiful experience. The beauty of God is indescribable, but Scripture tries anyway:

His glory is great through your help;
splendor and majesty you bestow on him.

　　　　　　　　　　　　—Psalm 21:5

Honor and majesty are before him;
　　strength and **beauty** are in his sanctuary.

　　　　　　　　　　　　—Psalm 96:6

On the glorious **splendor** of your majesty,
　　and on your wondrous works, I will meditate.

　　　　　　　　　　　　—Psalm 145:5

In that day the Lord of hosts will be a garland of glory,
　　and a diadem of **beauty**, to the remnant of his
　　people.

　　　　　　　　　　　　—Isaiah 28:5

These verses describe God as the very definition of the beauty we seek. God's beauty isn't a fading glamour, like the beauty of people on *People* magazine's list of the 100 most beautiful people. Yet God's beauty does have something in common with the beauty of Julia Roberts, Halle Berry, and Tom Cruise, and other glamorous celebrities. That something is *attractiveness*. We're drawn to God's truth, beauty, and goodness.

The trouble with beauty

God's beauty is not talked about as much as it should be. Perhaps Church leaders are not entirely comfortable with the notion of the beauty of God. In fact, our culture has more than a few biases against beauty. Consider the following prevailing beliefs.

Beauty is seen as useless and decorative

In a utilitarian age where the value of anything is measured by its usefulness, beauty is seen as mere frosting on the cake—pretty but not essential. But beauty cannot be reduced to that which is simply pretty or pleasant. Beauty is profound and deep and intimately connected with truth and goodness.

Beauty is simply in the eye of the beholder

Beauty is seen as a purely subjective reality, a matter of the whims and tastes of individuals. The fact is that some things are more beautiful than others. A sculpture by Donatello or a symphony by Mozart *is* more beautiful than a Precious Moments® figurine or a Justin Bieber song. What is needed is some training of the eye and ear. Author and preacher John Piper reminds us that "beauty must have a meaning that is larger and more permanent than personal quirks" (*Desiring God: Meditations of a Christian Hedonist*). God is not beautiful because he fits our style, taste, whims, or quirks. God's beauty is an objective reality. God told Moses, "I AM WHO I AM." (Exodus 3:14). God just is. Likewise, his beauty just is.

Beauty is not to be trusted

Beauty can be used for evil. Why are so many sinister spies portrayed as beautiful women in the movies? St. Paul warns that "even Satan disguises himself as an angel of light" (2 Corinthians 11:14). We do indeed need to be on the lookout for deception, but this doesn't mean that beauty can't be trusted. Claims of truth can also be deceptive. Many people are hypocrites. This does not mean that truth and goodness aren't real. We continue to pursue beauty, relying on discernment to judge when we are encountering true beauty or when we are being seduced by an imposter.

Beauty is the substance of God

Beauty is a doorway to the sacred. In his book *The Glory of the Lord: A Theological Aesthetics*, twentieth-century Catholic theologian Hans Urs von Balthasar writes:

> [I]f the form of [God's] glory—which mere thought can never simply banish—consists not only in awe, thankfulness, admiration, and submission, but also in joy, pleasure, and delight in God and in his splendor, if the form of his glory is determined precisely by his ability to transport us to joy and further determined by that joyous rapture itself: how could we *then* possibly dispense with the concept of the beautiful?

Von Balthasar reminds us that there are three kinds of literature in the Old Testament: the Law, the Prophets, and the Writings. The Law corresponds to our experience of God as *truth*. The Prophets correspond to our experience of God as *goodness*. The Writings (Psalms, Job, Proverbs, Song of Solomon, Ecclesiastes, Sirach, and Wisdom) correspond to our experience of God as *beauty*.

> We are not dealing here with a feeble, belated, and romantic transfiguration of a long-past and heroic golden era. We are witnessing the radiant drawing out into consciousness of the aesthetic dimension which is inherent in this unique dramatic action, a dimension which is the proper object of a theological aesthetics.

Von Balthasar is emphasizing that the concept of God as beautiful is not fluff—it is integral to our understanding of the very nature and substance of God and our relationship with him.

For Catholics, this notion of the beauty of God is the focus of the traditional Catholic practice of eucharistic adoration. In this prayer Catholics simply spend time sitting or kneeling in total silence, gazing at the consecrated Host which is the body of Christ displayed in an ornately adorned vessel called a monstrance. This prayer is called "adoration," since its focus is simply to adore the beauty of God's presence made real and visible in the Blessed Sacrament. The purpose of eucharistic adoration is to deepen our desire to be one with God's beauty. Prayer of adoration invites us to reflect on those qualities that make God beautiful so that we can live as a reflection of that same beauty.

Falling in love with God

We need to fall in love with God. When we fall in love, we tend to lose our grip on our own lives. And that's precisely the definition of conversion. When we fall in love with God, we let go of our own lives and center our lives on God's beauty, which haunts us in the most delightful ways. Our relationship with God needs passion. God wants to take us on a second honeymoon. That may sound strange until you take a look at this passage from Hosea in which God speaks of his unfaithful spouse, Israel, and tells his plan to put things right in their relationship.

> Therefore, I will now allure her,
>   and bring her into the wilderness,
>   and speak tenderly to her. . . .
> There she shall respond as in the days of her youth,
>   as at the time when she came out of the land of
>   Egypt.
> On that day, says the LORD, you will call me, "My
>   husband," and no longer will you call me,
>   "My Baal."
>
> —Hosea 2:14–16

The wilderness is where God and his Chosen People enjoyed their first honeymoon, immediately after God had led the Jewish people from slavery in Egypt to freedom. Now, years later, the fire has gone out of the relationship. Israel has strayed, seeking beauty in a new lover, the Canaanite god Baal. God will have none of it. He intends to seduce Israel, calling her back to the wilderness to reignite the passion that once fueled their relationship. Pretty hot stuff.

God desires us even more than we desire God. He longs to rekindle a love affair with each one of us. He longs to invite us into his beauty—the *beauty that we desire and need for spiritual wellness.*

Doorways to divine beauty

Seeing God face-to-face—experiencing the joy and excitement of his presence—leads us to encounter beauty in this world, which is a doorway to encountering God himself. God is revealing his beauty to us in so many ways each and every day. We need only to train our senses to find God in all things.

The key is to see the beauty all around us as a *reflection of God's beauty*. The world's beauty is not an end in itself. Adolph Hitler and his Nazi upper echelon appreciated works of art and classical music, but to them they were testaments to the superiority of the Aryan race and the Third Reich. Art and other beautiful things are doorways to divine beauty. Just as we offer grace in thanksgiving for good food, we need to offer grace in thanksgiving for beautiful music, beautiful works of art, and beautiful natural wonders.

Let's look at some of the ways that we can fill our lives with a deeper appreciation of God's beauty all around us.

The natural world

We start with the natural world that God created and filled with beauty. Architect Frank Lloyd Wright said, "I believe in God, only I spell it Nature." We literally need to stop and smell the roses in our everyday lives.

This is something children do quite naturally. I remember watching a T-ball game for five-year-olds at the park. The game suddenly stopped when the runner on second base, along with the shortstop and second baseman from the other team, gathered near the base to watch a little army of ants crawling. The children were oblivious to the game, much to the chagrin of the coach and parents, because they had found something far more interesting and beautiful to observe. We can appreciate these small gifts of nature all around us. Those of us who are urban creatures need to get outside more often.

We can take walks, exercise, do gardening, go camping, canoeing, bird watching, and fishing. We can also watch programs on television such as *Nature* on PBS, *Planet Earth* on the Discovery Channel, or the National Geographic Channel that explore and celebrate the beauty of nature.

Music

Aldous Huxley observed, "After silence, that which comes nearest to expressing the inexpressible is music." The book of Psalms is filled with references to praising God in song. Music lifts our minds and hearts. Its beauty transports us to a place where we experience the spiritual. The beating of a drum in tribal ritual and in contemporary men's groups lifts us out of the ordinary and into the realm of the spiritual.

I love classical music, but I believe that just about any form of music is capable of expressing beauty. Jazz, blues, rock, bluegrass, and soul can put us in touch with the spiritual, too. Some kinds of music are more beautiful than others, but God's taste in music is very eclectic. If you play a musical instrument, find God in your musical expressions. If you listen to music, let it stir your soul, lift your spirit, and bring you to a greater awareness of the beauty of God.

Visual arts

One of my favorite spiritual experiences is visiting the Art Institute of Chicago. I am no art connoisseur, but certain works of art can transport me. Pope Benedict XVI spoke of the power of art in one of his weekly general audiences in September, 2011:

> Art is like an open doorway to the infinite, toward a beauty and truth that go beyond everyday reality. A sculpture, a painting, a poem or a piece of music can

arouse a feeling of joy when it becomes apparent it is something more than just a chunk of marble, a canvas covered with colors, or words or notes on a page. It's something bigger, something that speaks and touches your heart; it carries a message and lifts the spirit.

Enjoy the visual arts—painting, drawing, sculpture, ceramics, photography, film and video, architecture, the performing arts, crafts, graphic design, fashion, and interior design. Know that God's first act of creation was visual art, when he uttered the words, "Let there be light."

Athleticism

My Dad used the word *beautiful* to describe the style of hockey that the Montreal Canadiens played in the 1950s and 1960s. He admired the fluid skating and flawless passing of Jean Beliveau, Maurice "Rocket" Richard, and Yvan "The Roadrunner" Cournoyer. (I hated the Canadiens because they always beat my beloved Chicago Blackhawks.) But my Dad was right. There is a beauty to the athleticism of sports. Just watch a slow-motion video of football highlights set to classical music. Or watch the Olympics, where athletes from all over the world achieve new heights and faster speeds. The experience of God in athleticism was perhaps best summed up by Olympic sprinter Eric Liddell who, in a famous line from the great movie *Chariots of Fire*, explained that, "I believe God made me for a purpose, but he also made me fast. And when I run I feel his pleasure."

If you are an athlete (even an occasional athlete), I hope you also feel God's pleasure in your athletic endeavors. If you enjoy watching sports as I do, don't just watch to see who wins. Appreciate the athleticism on display and let it inspire you to soar with the athletes to new heights where God's beauty is experienced.

Literature

Good literature possesses beauty. F. Scott Fitzgerald said that literature enables us to "discover that your longings are universal longing, that you're not lonely and isolated from anyone. You belong." Few things can transport us like a good story. Good literature entertains, educates, pleases, and conveys ideas. It is capable of penetrating and sparking the imagination, making it possible for the reader to awaken to the beauty of life. C. S. Lewis describes the power of literature saying, "Literature adds to reality, it does not simply describe it. It enriches the necessary competencies that daily life requires and provides; and in this respect, it irrigates the deserts that our lives have already become." Salman Rushdie writes, "Literature is where I go to explore the highest and lowest places in human society and in the human spirit, where I hope to find not absolute truth but the truth of the tale, of the imagination and of the heart."

Spirituality is fed by good literature, whether it is Christian or not. So read classic tales, short stories, poetry, novels, fiction and nonfiction, biographies—maybe even toss in a comic book now and then—anything that will inspire you to reflect on goodness, truth, and beauty.

This, of course, is not an exhaustive list of ways we can encounter beauty day to day. I encourage you to reflect on all the ways you consciously seek and encounter beauty in your life. Learn to recognize this beauty as a reflection of God's beauty, which is the object of our deepest and most passionate desires. This is a necessary key to strengthening your soul's immune system and finding spiritual wellness.

A last thought on beauty

In African-American churches it is common for preachers to do the following call and response with their congregation: "God is good!" *"All the time!"* "All the time!" *"God is good!"*

Let's shout, "God is beautiful!" *"All the time!"* "All the time!" *"God is beautiful!"*

KEY 7

Unleashing Your Imagination

What gives you heartburn?

I'm not talking about the bad kind of heartburn. I know all about that kind of heartburn. I grew up as the son of a pharmacist and worked for years in our family drugstore, dispensing remedies for bad heartburn. I'm talking about good heartburn—the kind you actively seek and desire. I'm talking about those things that set your heart on fire. If you find those things, you'll be on your way to spiritual wellness.

This is what two disciples found on the road to Emmaus in the Gospel of Luke. The men just witnessed the vicious and humiliating public execution of the leader they thought would change the world, and they are in the depths of despair. The dream is over. They are on their way to Emmaus, but there's nothing to see or do in Emmaus. The truth is, they are getting out of town fast. They want to escape the pain of Jerusalem.

On the road they encounter a stranger. Their despair clouds their minds and they don't recognize him as the risen Christ. Jesus listens to their story; then he challenges them to see things differently as he guides them through the Scriptures. Finally, when he breaks bread with them at the table, their eyes are opened and they recognize the risen Lord in their midst. Their first words are, "Were not our hearts burning within us while he was talking to us on the road?" (Luke 24:32). They had *heartburn,* and they were in no hurry to take Maalox! They had the kind of heartburn that you want to keep.

Back to our question: What gives *you* heartburn? What sparks a fire in your heart? What two sticks are you rubbing together in hopes of igniting such a fire? Answer that question, and you'll know where your spirituality is going. In his book *The Holy Longing,* Ronald Rolheiser says, "What we do with that fire, how we channel it, is our spirituality." Ultimately, spirituality is about the fire within.

A vision of something greater

Each of us walks around with a vision of a hoped-for reality—an alternate reality for ourselves, for those we love, for our community, for our world. In Ignatian spirituality this is called the *magis,* the Latin word meaning "more." We seek something more, something greater, a greater good. We can approach life as a contest to be won or as a mystery to be entered into. Without that drive for "the more," life is little more than a frustrating problem we can't seem to solve or an absurd game that we can't seem to win. With that drive for "the more," life becomes a mystery that enfolds us.

To be spiritual is to enter the realm of mystery—the more—and to see a reality that is hidden from plain sight. It is to acknowledge that there is more than meets the eye. To be spiritually alive means to cultivate a persistent awareness of "the more." Like those giant SETI (Search for Extra Terrestrial Intelligence) satellite dishes that search the cosmos for signs of alien life, our soul looks for the many ways that the spiritual realm overlaps the physical realm. Luckily, God is not hiding. His signs are numerous, yet they are often subtle. Fortunately, our souls are equipped to detect these signs.

Clear away distractions first

Life has an annoying ability to distract us just enough so that we forget to activate these functions of the soul. Here's a brief look at some of these problems.

Indifference

To be spiritual means to be attuned to others as well as to God. But life can make us indifferent and callous. The final episode of the television sitcom *Seinfeld* offers an illustration. In the show, Jerry, George, Elaine, and Kramer are arrested for breaking a Good Samaritan law in a small New England town. In typical *Seinfeld* fashion, the four of them stand idly by while a citizen is being carjacked. Jerry's comment, "That's a shame," epitomizes the characters' indifference. The trial proves that shallow indifference is a pattern in their lives. They cared very little for the things of ultimate significance. They had no depth, no commitment, no real emotion, no sentiment, and no growth. Instead, they were obsessed with the trivial, as when Jerry breaks up with his girlfriend because he finds it vexing that she eats her peas one at a time.

Indifference can creep into our lives. We may be very active and busy and yet be spiritually indifferent about issues of mercy and justice. The Christian humanist Dorothy Sayers said that indifference "believes in nothing, cares for nothing, seeks to know nothing, interferes with nothing, enjoys nothing, loves nothing, hates nothing, finds purpose in nothing, lives for nothing and remains alive only because there is nothing it would die for." In essence, there is no heartburn—no fire.

Distractions

In *The Seven Habits of Highly Effective People*, Stephen Covey suggests that we divide our activities into four quadrants.

- Quadrant I includes activities that are important and urgent.

- Quadrant II includes those that are important but not urgent.

- Quadrant III is for those activities that are not important but urgent.

- Quadrant IV is for things that are not important and not urgent.

Covey says that we spend way too much time in quadrants III and IV, dealing with things that are not all that important, even if some of them strike us as urgent. They are distractions: cell phone calls, text messages, Facebook updates, e-mails, reality shows, sports, idle chit-chat. Most of these items are not bad things, but they can multiply, in the way Tribbles multiplied on *Star Trek's Enterprise*, interfering with the ship's mission.

Philosopher Blaise Pascal describes the matter succinctly in his book *Pensées*:

> The only thing that consoles us for our miseries is diversion, and yet this is the greatest of our miseries. For it is this which principally hinders us from reflecting upon ourselves, and which makes us insensibly ruin ourselves.

Without this we should be in a state of weariness, and this weariness would spur us on to seek a more solid means of escaping from it. But diversion amuses us, and leads us, gradually and without ever adverting to it, to death.

Spiritual wellness thrives on quadrant II activities: important things that are not necessarily urgent. These would include things like prayer, exercise, planning and evaluating, true recreation, rest, seeking beauty, ongoing learning, and formation.

Cynicism

Sooner or later for most of us, our youthful idealism wanes in the face of life's constant bombardment of bad news. The twenty-four-hour news cycle wears us down. Lost idealism can become cynicism. In the Old Testament it is referred to as "grumbling." After the euphoria of escaping slavery in Egypt, the Israelites gradually lose their zeal for the journey to the Promised Land. Take a look at Exodus, chapters 15, 16, and 17, and you'll find the word *grumbling* (or *murmuring* or *complaining*, depending on the translation) appearing no less than ten times!

The Israelites had reason to complain. After all, they were living in the harsh desert with no food or water. We often have reason to grumble, too. But if grumbling leads to cynicism, we'll lose happiness, as will those who have to listen to us. *Spiritual wellness thrives on imagining possibilities*, while cynicism concludes there are none. Moses said that to grumble is to question God's presence, because if one truly believed in God's presence, one would see possibilities, even in the midst of despair. In his book *Barefoot Disciple: Walking the Way of Passionate Humility*, Stephen Cherry makes an important distinction between protesting and grumbling: "There are occasions when it is right to respond to sadness, disappointment or loss with protest. To protest is to commit to making a difference. Grumbling, on the other hand, is being content to create a miserable noise and create a negative atmosphere."

If anyone earned the right to grumble it would be St. Paul, as mentioned earlier. In return for his efforts to change the world, Paul was blinded, arrested, imprisoned, stoned, beaten, whipped, and shipwrecked. Rather than complaining about these things, he says, "Do all things without grumbling" (Philippians 2:14). Instead of complaining, he urges the Philippians to unleash their imagination: "Whatever is true, whatever is honorable, whatever is just, whatever is pure, whatever is pleasing, whatever is commendable, if there is any excellence and if there is anything worthy of praise, think about these things" (Philippians 4:8).

Relativism

History has seen enough violent conflicts perpetrated in the name of religion. Europe has had many of them. The attack on the United States on September 11, 2001, was purportedly done in the name of Islam (although any faithful Muslim will rightly deny that Islam condones violence). In response to violence in the name of religion, many people have concluded that religious differences are the cause of too many problems and should therefore be downplayed. This attitude is a big reason why Europe today is almost completely secular. It affects American attitudes toward religion as well.

This thinking leads to an attitude of relativism: nothing is true; everything is true. Relativism denies any absolute truth. It says, "Whatever you believe is right and no one can tell you otherwise." With regards to religion, relativism says that in the end, we all worship the same God anyway. Instead of learning to speak intelligently and with civility about religious differences, we ignore them and pretend that they do not exist. This spiritual vacuum where God is not to be talked about makes us reluctant to think about the greater realities of life. We shift the focus inward and think about ourselves. In our efforts to be politically correct and polite, we stuff God in the closet, like an embarrassingly outdated leisure suit.

The result is a spiritual malaise. Fr. Robert Barron, author of the *Catholicism* DVD series, offers this analogy. Picture a raging river where waters are flowing healthily between its firm banks. Those banks are absolute truths. They hold the waters and cause them to flow so mightily. Take away the banks and the water simply disperses every which way, eventually forming a lazy lake that quickly grows stale. A healthy spirituality is grounded in absolute truths. When various people lay claim to opposing or at least seemingly irreconcilable truths, the solution is not to abandon truth but to civilly discuss differences so that the ultimate truth can be arrived at by all.

Each of the above diversions—indifference, distractions, cynicism, and relativism—causes our spirit to experience what the fourth-century monk Evagrius of Pontus called the "noonday devil." This term means a lack of energy about things of ultimate significance, similar to the physical lethargy we often experience after lunch. Like Bill Murray's character in the movie *Groundhog Day*, we find that nothing new ever happens to us when we resist doing the real work it takes to build a true relationship. We find ourselves settling for less when our soul yearns for more.

Imagination is more important than knowledge

The remedy for the noon-day devil is a revived and renewed imagination. Active imagination—our capacity for perceiving more than meets the eye—is like "spiritual photosynthesis," transforming that which cannot be seen into real energy for the soul.

Imagination is often accused of being out of touch with reality. In reality, imagination is the capacity to see beyond reality to an alternate reality. Imagination is the key to navigating, deciphering, and transcending the reality that meets the eye so that we can recognize unseen reality. Imagination is not foolishness. Albert Einstein asserted that "imagination is more important than knowledge." When a young mother asked Einstein what she should read to her son so that he could grow up to be a brilliant thinker like him, he replied, "Fairy tales." When she asked what she should read him next, Einstein replied, "More fairy tales!" Einstein said, "When I examine myself and my methods of thought, I come to the conclusion that the gift of fantasy has meant more to me than any talent for abstract, positive thinking." In his essay "On Fairy-Stories," J. R. R. Tolkein wrote that fantasy (freeing oneself from the boundaries of seen reality) is "not a lower but a higher form of Art, indeed the most nearly pure form, and . . . the most potent."

Imagination is at the heart of the gospel message. If any part of the gospel could be called Jesus' core message, it would be the Sermon on the Mount, a lengthy discourse brimming with imaginative concepts climaxed in the Beatitudes. It takes great imagination to recognize the blessings of being poor, of peacemaking, of being meek, of mourning, of hungering for justice, and of being persecuted for righteousness sake. It takes great imagination to turn the other cheek, to love your enemies, and to pray for those who persecute you. Jesus tells us that this is the reality of the kingdom of God—a reality that is in our midst, albeit unseen. By his very existence—his incarnation—Jesus transformed this unseen reality into a seen reality.

Jesus not only preached about the kingdom of God, he literally embodied it. A well-known gospel verse, John 3:16, says, "For God so loved the world that he gave his only Son, so that everyone who believes in him may not perish but may have eternal life." We can paraphrase this to say, "For God *had such a great imagination*, that he sent his only Son . . ." Love requires great imagination. Spiritual wellness is all about the loving relationship we have with a personal God, not with some nebulous vapor or impersonal force. Spirituality is not something we dabble in. To dabble in spirituality would be as absurd as dabbling in marriage. In such a profound relationship, we dive in with every fiber of our being and commit ourselves to making it work. In marriage the risks are great, since we have no guarantee that our spouse will reciprocate with steadfast and unflinching faithfulness. With God, we can trust that he will be faithful. That does not remove the risk, however. Ultimately, we have to trust that the God who has shown such generous and faithful love throughout salvation history will do the same for us.

Learn the language of the soul

Jesus' wildly imaginative proclamation of the kingdom of God is an invitation to an indispensable *way of seeing*. Imagination is a prerequisite for hope. To be imaginative is to develop a way of approaching reality that brings us into contact with mystery. John Shea observes, "Thinking is the furniture and imagination is the room. We can rearrange the furniture all we want, but sometimes what we need is a larger room." The kingdom of God that Jesus proclaims is the larger room we need. In fact, Jesus compares the kingdom of God to a mansion with many rooms, "In my Father's house there are many dwelling places" (John 14:2). Imagination is the key to entering this mansion, and the language spoken in the mansion is a language of mystery. We need to learn this new language of imagination.

Words are not the primary form of expression in the language of imagination. The Spirit is more at home with other ways to communicate. Here are some of these ways.

Sign and symbol

Think about how Moses first encountered God. It was through the sign of a burning bush. Upon seeing this sign, Moses said, "I must turn aside and look at this great sight" (Exodus 3:3). Signs and symbols speak directly to the heart through the imagination.

Ritual

Rituals connect us with meaningful events in our past and ground us in the present, leading us confidently into the future. Rituals awaken a deeper level of consciousness within us—that place where the Spirit dwells.

Movement and gesture

One word: yoga. I'm not into yoga, but I get it. Our spirit is not a separate reality from our body. Spirit and body are conjoined; what happens to one affects the other. Sickness makes us sad and sadness can make us sick. Spiritual wellness depends on harmony between body and spirit, meaning that we don't have to be perfectly still in order to reach a spiritual state. In fact, quite the opposite is often true. Controlled, reverent, prayerful movements can bring about a corresponding prayerfulness of spirit.

Silence

I'll keep quiet on this one and let someone else speak. "Silence is God's first language; everything else is a poor translation. In order to hear that language, we must learn to be still and to rest in God" (Thomas Keating).

Song

Lucky for us, God loves music. Music and song can transport us to another state of mind. "O sing to the LORD a new song" says Psalm 96:1. This is only one of nearly one hundred references in the psalms to song and worship. When Israel was mired in exile in Babylon, one of the ways they expressed their despair was through their *refusal* to sing:

> By the rivers of Babylon—
>   there we sat down and there we wept
>   when we remembered Zion.
> On the willows there
>   we hung our harps.
> For there our captors
>   asked us for songs,
> and our tormentors asked for mirth, saying,
>   "Sing us one of the songs of Zion!"
> How could we sing the LORD's song
>   in a foreign land?
>
> —Psalm 137:1–4

Story and myth

Approximately one-third of the recorded sayings of Jesus are contained in parables. The man could tell a story. Stories create worlds. Jesus' stories tap into our imaginations, compelling us to consider the possibility of an alternate reality. John Shea says that "story is the most interesting and compelling of language forms. . . . Storytelling raises us out of the randomness of the moment and inserts us into a larger framework." That larger framework is the world of the Spirit.

The language of mystery gives us an alternate reality, which is the essence of the kingdom of God. If things were simply as they appeared, we would have no need for a spiritual life. Life's ultimate meaning is veiled and mysterious, so we nurture our spirit by incorporating the language of mystery into our soul's daily diet. This is precisely why I embrace Catholicism: at its best, it speaks a language of mystery that kindles a fire within my heart and compels me to seek "the more" that is the kingdom of God proclaimed by Jesus Christ.

Some ways to light the fire of imagination

How do we jump-start our imaginations? A good way is to exercise the right side of the brain, the place where imagination is strongest. The human brain has two hemispheres. Both sides think, but each side does so in a vastly different way. The left side tends to be more logical and analytical, while the right side tends to be more creative and imaginative. Here are some ways to get the imaginative juices in our right brain flowing:

- Turn off the television
- Read, especially fiction and biographies
- Focus on humor
- Draw or paint a picture
- Peruse works of art

- Work with your hands
- Listen to music and sing when possible
- Get a hobby
- Get regular exercise, eat right, and get enough sleep
- Break your patterns and be illogical on occasion
- Keep an idea notebook or write in a journal
- Attend theater
- Rearrange your work space/living space
- Meditate
- Do deep breathing
- Learn a new language
- Associate with creative people
- Cook or bake something creative
- Do some decorating/remodeling
- Travel or do armchair traveling
- Interact with children
- Play board games that require strategy

All of these things can awaken your imagination and spark the fire in your heart that fuels a healthy spirituality.

Since spiritual wellness is all about being aligned with the Spirit, we should ask, What is God fired up about? I think he is most fired up by selfless love. Mercy. Compassion. Justice. God's great imagination envisions a world in which the hungry are fed, the thirsty are given drink, the sick are tended to, the homeless are sheltered, the imprisoned are visited, the naked are clothed, and the estranged are welcomed. A healthy spirituality compels us to be present to people in need, offering them the possibility of seeing the presence of God, which is obstructed by the pain in their lives. Dorothy Day insisted that everything a baptized person should do every day should be directly or indirectly related to the corporal and spiritual works of mercy. She knew that God's fire could be found there. If you are looking for God—the goal of spirituality—these are the places to look. As the traditional Christian hymn *Ubi Caritas* reminds us: "Where charity and love prevail, there God is ever found."

The God we seek is on fire, has a mission, and invites you and me to be a part of it.

Imagine that.

Conclusion:
Spiritual Wellness
Equals Holiness

Does the name Frank Abignale Jr. ring a bell?

Leonardo DiCaprio played him in the film *Catch Me If You Can*. It's the story of Frank Abignale Jr., who was one of the biggest con men of all time. By the time he was twenty years old, Frank had conned millions of dollars out of companies and individuals by assuming fake identities: as an airline pilot, a doctor, an attorney, and an FBI agent. He was a terrific success as a phony, but he eventually grew tired of himself and began to loathe the empty and unhappy person he had become.

No one wants to be known as phony or a fake. Phonies or fakes take advantage of others and none of us enjoys being taken advantage of. This is especially true in relationships. We all hope and pray that we will find spouses and friends who are the real thing. We want to be around people who are *authentic*. Ultimately, that's what a healthy spirituality is all about—authenticity. Another word for that is *holiness*. For more than two thousand years countless numbers of Christians have sought to live lives of holiness by entering into a relationship with the most authentic person in human history: Jesus Christ.

Jesus is authentic. In the Nicene Creed we affirm that he is "God from God, light from light, true God from true God." We also say that he was "incarnate of the Virgin Mary and became man" and that he "suffered death . . . was crucified, died, and was buried." He is the real thing. He is authentic. And his love is authentic. We know this because he gave his life for us. Real love is unselfish and wants nothing in return. That's the kind of love that God offers to us. God's love is selfless and unconditional. He wants only to give to us.

That's what it means to be holy. God invites you to be holy as he is holy. Holiness doesn't mean that we have to be perfect. God is not calling us to be perfect; he calls us to be authentic. That means that we are called to love as God loves—unselfishly. Spiritual wellness does not mean perfection. It simply means that we are an authentic follower of Jesus.

This isn't easy. In our world it's easier to be phony or fake. Spiritual wellness means saying no to that phony stuff, which usually looks good and feels good on the surface, but which ultimately causes us to "miss the mark" (that's the literal meaning of the word *sin*.) It's no coincidence that at Baptism—the ritual that begins our journey toward spiritual wellness—the first question asked by the priest is: "Do you reject Satan, and all his works, and all his empty promises?" The journey to holiness begins with the sobering reminder that, without intervention, we will continue to hopelessly miss the mark. Baptism is the intervention we need. There is no quick fix or magic involved. It is simply the watershed moment in our lives when we admit that we need help and open ourselves up to the grace that heals. That's why Catholics so often renew our baptismal promises at Mass. We need to frequently reject Satan because he doesn't go away.

This book is my attempt to promote authenticity. I hope to make holiness accessible to the average person since, according to Catholic teaching, we are *all* called to holiness. The seven keys to spiritual wellness offered here are tried-and-true strategies that flow from the Christian tradition. This book is really about the seven deadly sins and the seven virtues that are the antidotes for the deadly sins. This book is an example of putting old wine in new wineskins. It's a new package for something that has been taught for centuries by countless numbers of people before me. Here are the traditional seven deadly sins and curative virtues, along with my "new wineskins."

Deadly Sin	Curative Virtue	Key to Spiritual Wellness	Key Question
Pride	Humility	Seeing Yourself as You Really Are	Who's your court jester?
Envy	Charity	Actively Seeking the Good of Others	What do you have that cannot be taken away?
Anger	Gentleness/ Prudence	Thinking Before Acting	Is that your final answer?
Greed	Generosity	Holding on Loosely	What's your security blanket?
Gluttony	Temperance	Recognizing and Setting Limits	What scratches your itch?
Lust	Chastity	Seeking Beauty	Where is your dream vacation spot?
Sloth	Zeal	Unleashing Your Imagination	What gives you heartburn?

I purposely chose not to use the terms "seven deadly sins" and "virtues" throughout this book. These terms carry a lot of religious baggage and also come across as very "churchy" and "preachy." People are no longer afraid of sin, even if you call those sins *deadly*. Furthermore, the Catholic Church's moral authority and credibility in preaching about sin has been severely damaged by the Church's own sinfulness, shown in the sexual abuse crisis perpetrated by priests and covered up by bishops. People today are not eager to hear the Church preach about sin while mired so deeply in her own.

Instead, I chose to tap into the wisdom of Church tradition by giving us something to say yes to, instead of repeating what we need to say no to. I repackaged these traditional teachings in a way that speaks to today's modern spiritual hunger—the spiritual hunger that drives countless people to seek spiritual nourishment outside of institutional religion.

I observed this phenomenon firsthand a few years ago when I encountered something offered on the Internet. Oprah Winfrey teamed up with self-proclaimed spiritual guru Eckhart Tolle to offer an online "course" in spirituality that attracted millions of people. I was astounded and saddened when the first "Skyper" to the program identified herself as a Catholic. She said that she liked Tolle and that she had never seen Catholicism as a spiritual path. I wanted to jump through the computer screen and "save her" from Tolle's vapid spirituality. I wanted to show her how her Catholic faith offers a treasure trove of spirituality. (I have read Tolle's book *A New Earth* and can assure you that, except for the parts that are little more than refried Buddhism, it is indeed vapid and lifeless.)

This woman is not alone. By striving to be precise in its teachings, the Catholic Church has developed a legalistic approach to the life of faith that doesn't draw people to experience the mysterious and ineffable God. Don't get me wrong. The dogma and doctrine of Catholicism are important, but only to the extent that they bring us deeper into an experience of the incomprehensible God. Too many Catholics are being taught that the key to salvation is to "abide by the rules," something that Rev. Robert Barron says is akin to teaching someone to love baseball by giving them the rule book and telling them to learn it. The rules are important in baseball, but you learn to love the game by playing it, watching it, and learning the rules along the way. In the same way, we know God by falling in love with Jesus first and foremost, and then live in a way that establishes boundaries to guide and protect that love.

I began this book by saying, "Unfortunately, Christianity has come to be seen by many as less than a spiritual path and more as a code of ethics." I'd like to conclude by emphasizing this again. People are hungry for spirituality. They long to live in a way that recognizes and connects with God's grace on a regular basis and in ordinary things. I pray that these seven keys I have outlined will help you avoid things that make you miss the mark (sin), and help you develop healthy habits (virtues) that will lead you to be an authentic follower of Jesus who finds God in all things.

P. S. By the way, the story of Frank Abignale Jr. has a good ending. He served time in prison, but he eventually became a legitimate and successful businessman, consulting banks, corporations, and even the FBI on how to detect phonies, as he used to be. He's doing what many catechists do for the people they teach: helping them learn the difference between what's phony and fake, between what's real and authentic. May *you* choose the real thing—Jesus Christ. May you always be his authentic follower and, in following him, find spiritual wellness all the days of your life.

Bibliography

Anderson, Douglas A. and Flieger, Verlyn, eds. *Tolkein on Fairy-Stories.* London and New York: HarperCollins, 2008.

Barron, Robert. *The Strangest Way: Walking the Christian Path.* Maryknoll, New York: Orbis Books, 2002.

Bennett, William, ed. *The Book of Virtues: A Treasury of Great Moral Stories.* New York: Simon and Schuster Paperbacks, 1993.

Brueggemann, Walter. *Cadences of Home: Preaching among Exiles.* Louisville, KY: Westminster John Knox Press, 1997.

Capps, Donald. *Deadly Sins and Saving Virtues.* Eugene, OR: Wipf and Stock Publishers, 1987.

Cherry, Stephen. *Barefoot Disciple: Walking the Way of Passionate Humility.* London and New York: Continuum, 2011.

Collins, Patrick W. *More Than Meets the Eye: Ritual and Parish Liturgy.* New York/Ramsey: Paulist Press, 1983.

Covey, Stephen R. *The Seven Habits of Highly Effective People: Powerful Lessons in Personal Change.* New York: Fireside, 1989.

Dean, Kenda Creasy. *Almost Christian: What the Faith of Our Teenagers Is Telling the American Church.* Oxford: Oxford University Press, 2010.

DeYoung, Rebecca Konyndyk. *Glittering Vices: A New Look at the Seven Deadly Sins and Their Remedies.* Grand Rapids, MI: Brazos Press, 2009.

Eldredge, John. *The Journey of Desire: Searching for the Life We've Only Dreamed Of.* Nashville, TN: Thomas Nelson Publishers, 2000.

Eliade, Mircea. *Rites and Symbols of Initiation: The Mysteries of Birth and Rebirth.* New York: Spring Publications, 2009.

Fessio, Joseph and John Riches, eds. *The Glory of the Lord: A Theological Aesthetics by Hans Urs von Balthasar. Vol.1: Seeing the Form.* Translated by Erasmo Leiva-Merikakis. San Francisco and New York: Ignatius Press and Crossroad Publications, 1982.

Foster, Richard J. *Freedom of Simplicity: Finding Harmony in a Complex World.* New York: HarperOne, 2005.

Grey, Jane. "Philosophy Essay on Truth, Goodness, and Beauty Part III: The Beauty of Holiness", 2009. Accessed at http://janegrey.hubpages.com/hub/Truth--Goodness--and-Beauty-Part-III-The-Beauty-of-Holiness.

Hatherley, Paul. *Expressing Love, Pursuing Truth, Experiencing Beauty: Timeless Steps to the Ultimate Satisfaction—A Meaningful Life.* Bloomington, IN: Balboa Press, 2011.

Keating, Thomas. *Divine Therapy and Addiction: Centering Prayer and the Twelve Steps.* Brooklyn, NY: Lantern Books, 2009.

Manney, Jim. *A Simple, Life-Changing Prayer: Discovering the Power of Saint Ignatius Loyola's Examen.* Chicago: Loyola Press, 2011.

O'Donohue, John. *Beauty: The Invisible Embrace.* New York: Harper Perennial, 2004.

Pascal, Blaise. *Pensées.* A. J. Krailsheimer, trans. New York: Penguin, 1985.

Piper, John. *Desiring God: Meditations of a Christian Hedonist.* Colorado Springs, CO: Multnomah Books, 2011.

Powell, John. *Fully Human, Fully Alive: A New Life Through a New Vision.* Niles, IL: Argus Communications, 1976.

Prothero, Stephen. *Religious Literacy: What Every American Needs to Know—And Doesn't.* San Francisco: HarperOne, 2007.

Rite of Christian Initiation of Adults: Study Edition. International Commission on English in the Liturgy and Bishop's Committee on the Liturgy, National Conference of Catholic Bishops. Chicago: Liturgy Training Publications, 1988.

Rohr, Richard and Martos, Joseph. *The Great Themes of Scripture: Old Testament.* Cincinnati, OH: St. Messenger Press, 1987.

Rolheiser, Ronald. *The Holy Longing: The Search for a Christian Spirituality.* New York: Doubleday, 1999.

Sanford, John A. *Ministry Burnout.* New York/Ramsey: Paulist Press, 1982.

Seven Deadly Sins, Seven Lively Virtues. DVD. Word on Fire, 2007.

Shea, John. *An Experience Named Spirit.* Allen, TX: Thomas More, 1983.

Shea, John. *Stories of Faith.* Chicago: Thomas More, 1980.

Sherry, Patrick. *Spirit and Beauty.* Second edition. London: SCM Press, 2002.

Taylor, Daniel. *The Myth of Certainty: Trusting God, Asking Questions, Taking Risks.* Grand Rapids, MI: Zondervan Publishing House, 1992.

Tolle, Eckhart. *A New Earth: Awakening to Your Life's Purpose.* New York: Plume, 2005.

Tomlin, Graham. *The Seven Deadly Sins and How to Overcome Them.* Oxford: Lion Books, 2007.

Westley, Dick. *Redemptive Intimacy: A New Perspective Journey to Adult Faith.* Mystic, CT: Twenty-Third Publications, 1981.

Wiesel, Elie. *First Person Singular.* DVD. PBS, 2002.

Wilken, Robert Louis. *The Spirit of Early Christian Thought: Seeking the Face of God.* New Haven and London: Yale University Press, 2003.

Acknowledgments

I am deeply grateful to the following people who have inspired, encouraged, and enabled me to undertake and complete this book: Joe Durepos, Maureen Kuhn, Jim Manney, Kathleen Suzuki, the Society of Jesus (the Jesuits), my brother Tom, and my wife, Jo.

Also by Joe Paprocki

Practice Makes Catholic
Moving from a Learned Faith
to a Lived Faith

$9.95 • Pb • 3322-7

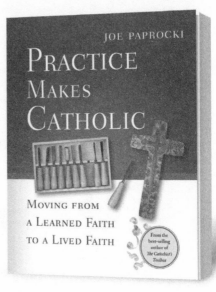

In *Practice Makes Catholic*,
Paprocki addresses the
all-important "why" of
many Catholic practices
by articulating five key
characteristics that form
our Catholic identity: a
sense of sacramentality,
a commitment to
community, a respect for the dignity of human life and
commitment to justice, a reverence for Tradition, and
a disposition to faith and hope rather than despair.
Under each of these categories, he explores and explains
multiple Catholic practices, then describes how following
each one can make a profound difference in our faith and
in our lives.

Informative and inviting, *Practice Makes Catholic* is the
perfect resource for RCIA candidates and their sponsors, for
Catholics returning to the faith, and for all Catholics who
want to get to the heart of what their faith is really about.

Also by Joe Paprocki

The Catechist's Toolbox
How to Thrive as a Religious
Education Teacher

$9.95 • Pb • 2451-5

Also available in Spanish
$9.95 • Pb • 2767-7

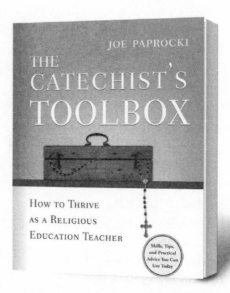

Written specifically
for any catechist who
is new to the job or has
never had any formal
training, *The Catechist's
Toolbox* features an
invaluable collection of
catechetical tips, techniques, methodologies, and advice.
Throughout the book, master teacher Joe Paprocki
shares the wisdom he has gleaned in his two decades as
a catechist, high school teacher, and religious educator.
Employing the metaphor of a homeowner's toolbox,
Paprocki explains how a new catechist is like a do-it-
yourself builder who needs the right collection of tools to
do the job; he then explains what the tools are, what they
can do, and how to use them skillfully and effectively.

To order: call 800-621-1008, visit www.loyolapress.com/store,
or visit your local bookseller.

Also by Joe Paprocki

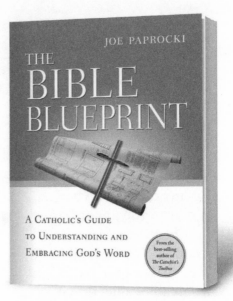

The Bible Blueprint
A Catholic's Guide to Understanding and Embracing God's Word

$9.95 • Pb • 2898-8

Also available in Spanish
$9.95 • Pb • 2858-2

In *The Bible Blueprint*, best-selling author Joe Paprocki makes understanding the Bible not only easy for the person in the pew, but downright fun! Using witty cartoons, thought-provoking sidebars, and short quizzes to supplement his easy-to-grasp teachings on the Bible, Paprocki guides lay Catholics to a solid understanding of the structure, organization, and purpose of God's Word.

Among numerous other topics, Paprocki covers the different genres of biblical writing, key figures in biblical history, and the methods that Catholics rely on to interpret the Bible.

Also by Joe Paprocki

A Well-Built Faith
A Catholic's Guide to Knowing
and Sharing What We Believe

$9.95 • Pb • 2757-8

Also available in Spanish
$9.95 • Pb • 3299-2

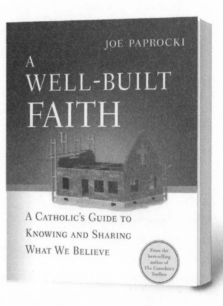

A Well-Built Faith—
creatively developed
around a construction
theme—makes it easy
for Catholics to know
what they believe and to
feel confident in sharing
those beliefs. This 18-chapter book by master teacher Joe
Paprocki follows the structure of the four pillars of the
Catechism of the Catholic Church (Creed, Sacraments,
Morality, and Prayer), making it a wonderful resource for
learning about and teaching the Catholic faith. Highly
informative and very fun at the same time, *A Well-Built
Faith* is a must-have tool for developing the Catholic
faith.

Also by Joe Paprocki

Living the Mass
How One Hour a Week
Can Change Your Life

Fr. Dominic Grassi and Joe Paprocki

$13.95 • Pb • 3614-3

Also available in Spanish August 2012!
$13.95 • Pb • 3758-4

In this revised edition of *Living the Mass*, which takes into account the changes in the new *Roman Missal*, Grassi and Paprocki thoughtfully explain how each part of the Mass relates to our baptismal call, effectively closing the gap between Sunday Mass and the rest of the week.

Ideal for the countless Catholics who attend Mass simply out of habit, for the many who haven't been to Mass in awhile, or for anyone who desires to join the Catholic Church, *Living the Mass* compellingly demonstrates how the one hour spent at Mass on Sunday can truly transform how we think and act the other 167 hours of the week.

To order: call 800-621-1008, visit www.loyolapress.com/store, or visit your local bookseller.